PRAISE FOR W
TH

"Kathy is an amazing writer! She offers a clear path to writing devotionals that make an impact. Anyone considering devotional writing should get a copy of her book."
Kathleen M. Bornarth, M.A., M.P.C
President, National Association of Christian Journal Writers

"Clear, concise, doable. Truthfully, I wasn't expecting to need this book. However, after reading it, I'm now inspired to write devotionals. With Kathy's guidance, I'm confident that I too can write devotionals that stick. Her method is clearly stated and easy to understand. I'm a member of a Christian author group, and have recommended that others get their eyes on this book!"
Kim Steadman, writer

"A must-read! I have read many books on writing but this one is foremost the best. The author covered every aspect of writing."
Pam, R., writer

"This book fills a very specific need in a very specific niche for writing. I would heartily recommend to all kinds of writers, not just ones who are looking to write devotionals. There is so much good, practical advice in here that all writers can benefit from many of these pointers. We should all desire for our writing, whether fiction or non-fiction or devotional, to be sticky with our readers."
David Wiley, author

"Amazing and innovative - one of the best tools I've seen for Christian devotionals. This book is a must-have for any writer's library."
Amazon reviewer

"Kathy Widenhouse has finally done something few if any have ever done: write a book about writing that actually holds your interest and teaches you easy to apply practical principles that actually work! This book may be focused on writing devotionals but the steps can easily be transferred into other forms of writing. She uses scripture to help readers see biblical truth and direction as they prepare to be an effective writer, which goes to the heart of why someone would be writing devotionals to begin with. Well done!"
Amazon reviewer

"I was directed to this book by a friend, and I am so very glad I now have it. It is just the thing for the writer getting started writing devotionals or blog posts on Biblical themes. For those who have been writing for some time, it is a great mirror to hold up to your work for assessment. It will make your writing more impactful; efficiently utilized, it will make your work sparkle. All Christians readily acknowledge Jesus' use of short stories - what we often overlook is how sticky they were. To be an effective writer today is to deliver the message in a way that sticks. Kathy Widenhouse brings it home in a very engaging style."
R. McBurnett

"I've been an on and off again blogger and journal enthusiast for many years. Little did I know that *Writing Devotionals that Stick* would be so timely in my life, informative, full of usable ideas and

realistically helpful starting (or in my case, restarting) points for those days when you just can't quite get on paper what's in your heart. If you're looking to become a better devotional writer or starting out for the first time, Kathy takes you from looking for ideas all the way to getting your point across to your target audience in the easy to read, informative and fun book."
Stephanie C., blogger

"Sticky – in the very best way! A practical guide for anyone wanting to be more effective in their writing! Kathy's simple, practical principles (The Tape Principle & SAM) make the advice here 'stick' in the reader's memory. This book offers a fresh perspective, based on scriptural illustrations, that you can apply to writing devotionals and preparing any type of lesson, making those lessons so much more 'stickable' for the learner or reader... and isn't that the goal for both writers & teachers? Great job!"
Tracey R. Ernst, teacher

"This book stuck to me! It's written in such a way that it communicates clear steps to the beginning writer as well as uncover gold nuggets for the seasoned devotional writer, too. Kathy uncovers the traps that many writers fall into and guides them in a clear, concise manner to unlock their potential."
Bryan C. Bradshaw, pastor

"This book is an extremely thoughtful, biblically based guide to devotional writing. Kathy provides a clear path from idea gathering to final 'sticky' product. A wonderful resource for anyone wishing to write effective devotionals to share personal experiences and insights from God."
Deb Gerber, teacher and mom

WRITING DEVOTIONALS THAT STICK

A STEP-BY-STEP GUIDE FOR WRITING THIS
UNIQUE GENRE FOR TODAY'S BUSY READERS

KATHY WIDENHOUSE

WRITING DEVOTIONALS THAT STICK

A Step-By-Step Guide to Writing This Unique Genre For Today's Busy Readers

© 2016 Kathy Widenhouse

ISBN: 978-1-5208-2227-3

Cover Design: James, aka Humble Nations at GoOnWrite.com

Published in the United States of America

To Brett
who has steadfastly encouraged me and grown with me.

CONTENTS

INTRODUCTION

In today's hectic and harried world, people need to experience God's presence more than ever.

We are distracted and overwhelmed, barraged by dozens of messages every hour and every day.

And many have lost hope.

Whether it's because we are busy and overextended, or because we live in perilous times, people struggle to see God move in their lives. We long for peace. We hunger to have a relationship with God and live in confident assurance, yet we struggle to see His activity among us.

But God IS active and moving.

If you've picked up a book about writing devotionals, there's a good chance you want to share with people how you have seen God move. You want to inspire them and give them hope.

That's great! And that's what this book is designed to do.

Writing Devotionals That Stick shows you step-by-step how to identify a truth about God from your daily life and write it in a format that will stick with today's busy readers.

I've been writing devotional material for over 25 years, first for a class at church and then as a way to begin writing for the Christian market. As I grew as a writer, I began writing books of devotionals, weekly devotionals for blogs, online devotionals, devotionals for clients ... for pre-teen girls and corporate leaders and pregnant women and youth group leaders ...

Over and over, it has been amazing to watch what happens.

As people read a devotional, they see an illustration of a biblical truth from daily life. A light bulb goes on. They discover a way to put the principle into practice in their lives. It sticks. And they grow!

Devotionals are a unique genre — a short piece of biblical inspiration wrapped in an illustration with a takeaway. And they are everywhere, both written and spoken: online, in your inbox, on your iPhone, in books   even at the start of church meetings and leadership seminars.

It is precisely their length that makes devotionals so powerful for today's on-the-go readers. A good devotional gives your reader a snippet to mull over. It stays with the reader. She'll think about it in the grocery line. He'll mull it over when walking to the coffee break room.

When you give readers good stuff for their spiritual "hard drive" — stuff that sticks — their minds will call it back up during the day or as they need it.

Anybody can write a devotional. That's the beauty of writing them ... yet also a danger.

Because they don't always stick.

Yours can.

You Can Write For This Unique Genre

Leaders, entrepreneurs, students, moms, professionals, writers, and many others who want to share their experiences with God have learned to write sticky devotionals by using the principles found in this book.

Think back to a meaningful spiritual truth you've lived by. How did that truth get into your heart?

Nine times out of ten, you will recall an illustration from a pastor, a writer, or an example from a friend. That example stuck in your mind. You mulled it over and finally said, "That's like God!" That illustration or anecdote or startling thought or fact STUCK with you. You return to it in your mind again and again.

You may even share it with other people as a way of explaining a spiritual truth.

That's what happened to Mike H. of California. He had ideas and examples galore from his decades of walking with God, but he struggled first with connecting them to scripture and second in being too verbose. His readers got lost.

But once Mike began to understand and use the principles that make a devotional stick, he was able to use them. Today he writes devotionals for his nonprofit's website and its regular emails. "I get all kinds of feedback about how these devotionals help our followers grow," says Mike.

A Promise to You

God has given you a desire to share insight about Him with others. This book helps you identify the insight God has given you in your everyday life and then structure that insight in a way that they can receive it, remember it, and use it.

The bottom line: If you practice the steps in this book, you'll be able to write for this unique genre in a way that stays with your busy, distracted readers. Your devotionals will stick.

And when they stick, you help people grow. Can there be anything more gratifying?

Don't Wait

God reminds us to "Guard what has been entrusted to you" (1 Timothy 6:20, NLT). He has entrusted you with a desire to write about your life experiences and insight into His Word by writing devotionals.

How sad it would be to be called to write devotionals, but have little understanding how to do so. Or to write down those experiences, but miss the impact you might have because you didn't know a few simple ways to make them stick.

But keep reading and you won't miss out on that opportunity. The steps in this book are quite simple. They have been used to create hundreds of devotionals that stick to readers. Each chapter offers you a new insight, principle, or tip to use as you write. Practice them and you'll improve your ability to write devotionals that stick and help others grow.

Get started now.

GETTING STARTED

1

GETTING TERMS STRAIGHT

FIRST, WE NEED TO TAKE CARE OF SOME HOUSEKEEPING. Let's get on the same page with our lingo.

The word "devotional" has become a catch-all term among people of faith.

So when it comes to a book about writing devotionals, it's helpful to have clarity about the word from the start.

What a Devotional Is

In faith circles, the word "devotional" can have at least three meanings, all mistakenly used interchangeably. You've probably heard the following — or at least a variation:

"I'm reading a devotional from this devotional during my devotional."

Uh ... confusing, right?

Meaning #1: "Devotional" is used to refer to a time

You may use the term "devotional" when you talk about the time you set apart to pray, read the Bible, and meditate, as in "I'm reading a devotional from this devotional during my **devotional**."

In this book, I'll refer to this time as "devotions" as a way to respect the different kinds of activities we use as we spend time with God.

Like this: "I'm reading a devotional from this devotional during my **devotions**."

Meaning #2: "Devotional" is used to refer to a collection

A "devotional" is a word that describes a collection of reading material, as in "I'm reading a devotional from this **devotional** during my devotions."

Used this way, "devotional" is a set of short pieces of inspiration. Each piece in the group is designed to be read as a stand-alone unit, one at a time. Many devotional collections, whether put together in books, magazines, or an online series, follow a theme or are structured to be used during a period of time, as in a "Christmas devotional book" (to be used during Advent) or "devotional book for mothers-to-be" (to be used during pregnancy.)

In this book, I'll refer to these resources as "devotional book," "devotional magazine," or "devotional collection."

Like this: "I'm reading a devotional from this **devotional book** during my devotions."

Meaning #3: "Devotional" is used to refer to a single piece of inspiration

It is common to reference a "devotional" as one unit from a collection, as in "I'm reading a **devotional** from this devotional during my devotional."

This is the way in which I use term "devotional" in this book. A devotional is single, short, written (or verbal) work. I'll even occasionally refer to it as a "devo," using the abbreviated term that's so popular with students — just for variety.

Like this: "I'm reading a **devotional (devo)** from this devotional book during my devotions."

So ... what is it?

What exactly is a devotional?

A devotional is a short, inspiring illustration with a biblical takeaway.

It sounds so simple. And it is.

A devotional is a unique genre, structured in three distinct parts (scripture, illustration, and a takeaway).

Its length is short. Its content inspires you in your walk of faith.

What A Devotional Is Not

Because of their length, devotionals can get a bad rap. More than one well-meaning leader has dismissed devotionals as too short and too superficial to have much impact on a person's journey of faith.

But that attitude implies that a devotional or any other piece of inspirational writing (apart from the Bible) can be the end-all and be-all for growth in the Christian life.

A devotional is simply one device to use to help you grow in your journey of faith.

You can better understand a devotional's function by thinking of a tool box. The box is filled with pieces of equipment and devices to help you do a job. Different tools in the Christ-follower's tool box fill different functions, but work together in faith building: sermons, individual prayer, worship, serving, giving, acts of mercy, Bible study, classes, personal Bible reading, articles, faith sharing, small groups, books, and (yes) devotionals ...

You don't expect a small hammer to cut down a 60-foot tree. You use a chain saw instead.

A devotional is not designed to do heavy lifting in the spiritual journey, nor is a devotional meant to be the centerpiece of guidance in a reader's walk of faith. Those tasks are better left to Bible study, in-depth teaching, a meaningful prayer life — the power saws in the tool box.

Of course, God can use whatever means He chooses to do heavy spiritual lifting.

But by design, a devotional has a different job to do. Its brevity and single focus make this form a unique and useful device, much like a small hammer or a match or a piece of flint. If used properly, a devotional can complete one small task. It can create a spiritual spark. That spark can drive the reader's next step.

The Christian life is a series of small steps, taken moment by moment and day after day. Therein lies the impact of a devotional: it touches the heart of a reader in life's daily moments and allows him to take one next step of faith.

One spark — from your devotional — becomes a pivot point in a reader's life of faith.

That's why it's important that devotionals stick.

2

GETTING STICKY

IN THIS BOOK, YOU'LL LEARN THE MECHANICS OF WRITING A devotional — a short, inspiring illustration with a biblical takeaway.

But you'll also learn how to write your message in a way that sticks with today's busy, distracted readers.

Let's use an everyday illustration to clarify.

On a notepad, you jot down the name of an item you need to remember to pick up at the store. Then you reach over to your tape dispenser and pull off a piece of tape. You attach one end of the piece of tape onto the paper and then press the other end of it onto the front of your refrigerator.

It sticks.

Adhesive tape is such an ordinary product that you may not stop to think about how it works. You simply use it.

But leaving chemistry aside, let's consider what happens here. In order for an item to stick to another item, two conditions need to be met. One item must be sticky — that is, have adhesive properties. The other item needs to be compatible — stickable — in order for the adhesive item to attach to it.

Our stick-the-note-on-the-fridge scenario works because the players are either sticky or stickable.

- The adhesive on the tape is sticky.
- The piece of paper and the refrigerator are stickable.

When it comes to writing devotionals, the principle is the same. I call it The Tape Principle. In order for a message with a biblical truth to stay with a reader, the players must be either stickable or sticky.

- The writer is stickable: his heart is positioned to hear and record truth from God.
- The reader is stickable: she is positioned to receive truth.
- The content is sticky: truth is presented so the reader can relate to it and understand it.

Getting Stickable and Sticky

When you are a stickable writer, your heart is positioned to hear from God and then record what you receive.

But you also understand your reader's stickability and you're able to format the truth in content that sticks to the reader.

This book explains all three of these players:

1. The writer (you!)
2. The reader
3. The content.

It shows you how to be a stickable writer. It helps you to understand ways that readers are stickable. And it shows you how to write sticky devotional content for them. For a devotional to be effective, all three players need to be stickable or sticky.

Throughout this book, we'll keep coming back to The Tape Principle.

It's a principle you can use as a self-check as you write devotionals. Always ask: Am I stickable? What's the writer's stickablity? Is this content sticky?

Let's look first at you.

PART 1: STICKABLE WRITERS

3

STICKY DEVOS START WITH YOU

THERE IS A BEAUTIFUL PASSAGE TUCKED AWAY IN THE OLD Testament book of Habakkuk that outlines the process of writing devotionals — a process that provides the foundation for this book.

"Write the vision; make it plain on tablets, so he may run who reads it" (Habakkuk 2:2).

The Writer Received a Blueprint

Habakkuk was a prophet. Like you and me, he lived in perilous times.

It was 7th century BC. Confusion and conflict reigned. The northern kingdom of Israel had been conquered by neighboring Assyria. Now, Habakkuk feared that enemies would attack and overtake the southern kingdom of Judah.

Habakkuk conversed with God on behalf of the Hebrew people about the escalating tension and violence, openly questioning God's presence and movement.

Those conversations are recorded in his book, Habakkuk,

which is just three chapters long. There God reveals an insight to Habakkuk which confirms the prophet's fears: Judah, the southern kingdom, was to be invaded by Babylon.

God also told Habakkuk what to do with that information: "Write the vision; make it plain ... so he may run who reads it."

Habakkuk was to write down the information he received from God, using tablets, which in Bible times were set in public places. This way, as people passed by they could read the information and act on it.

God's instructions to Habakkuk are a practical writing blueprint for you and me to follow today.

The Process Starts with the Writer

God's instructions identify three players in this process (Sound familiar? The Tape Principle has three players, too):

1. The writer: Habakkuk
2. The readers: the people who would read the information
3. The content: the revelation

In this book, we will look at each of these players and how God used them with Habakkuk in the writing process. How were they stickable or sticky?

Then we will apply that information to writing devotionals.

God's instructions are addressed to the first of these players — Habakkuk, the writer. As writers, you and I can take to heart these instructions.

What To Do

God gave Habakkuk a clear mandate to share what he has learned: "Write the vision." While it can be tempting to sail along through life and not listen or take note of the wisdom God imparts, that is not God's call on a writer's life. Like Habakkuk, you are to be open to how God speaks to you. You are to wrestle with what He shares with you so you can discern nuggets of truth. God's instructions are clear: don't let the insight you receive fall into oblivion. It is this step in the process — being a stickable writer — that we will discuss in more depth in this section.

Who to Write For

"So he may run who reads it." We write content to provide one way for others to absorb God's truth as it crosses their path, their desk, or their inbox. You need to know how your readership can receive this information so you can write it to make it stick. How readers use the truth you share is their responsibility. Yours is make it available and stickable, which we will address in Chapter 9.

How to Write It

When you are entrusted with a revelation or truth or vision or insight from God, it is incumbent upon you to communicate it in a way that others can understand it. You are to explain it clearly — to "make it plain." You will read how to do so in Chapters 10-16.

God's blueprint is clear: writing devotionals that stick does not start with the content. It does not start with the structure or mechanics of the devotional. It does not start with the reader.

It starts with the writer — a writer who is ready to hear what God has to say.

What Makes a Writer Stickable

You need to be a "ready writer" — one who is ready to let God's truth stick in his mind and to his heart.

For now, think about how Habakkuk positioned himself. He was aware of his surroundings. He listened to God. His heart was tender towards the things of God and he had concern for his people. He discussed his deepest fears honestly with God. And once he heard God's message, he wrote it — clearly — and made it available to readers.

Pay attention to life as it happens around you. Talk with God about it and hear what He has to say. He will help you grasp the vision of truth that He reveals. And be ready to write it plainly so others can read it.

Readiness to see, readiness to hear, and readiness to process what God's says: being ready to do those things makes you stickable.

4

HOW STICKABLE WRITERS GET IDEAS

ONE PART OF THE WRITING PROCESS STUMPS MOST OF US, NO matter who you are: a leader who uses devotionals in your ministry ... a writer who is eager to add "devotionals" to your can-do list ... a Christ-follower who wants to record what God is teaching you so you can share it with others ... or someone who wants to write devotionals for any other reason.

The stumbling block is pre-writing.

Pre-writing is the work you do before you work on any writing project. In this case, it's the work you do before you write the devotional.

Pre-writing creates an obstacle because we wrongly believe that if we are not typing or scribbling or crossing out or adding words — when we're not "officially" engaged in the physical act of writing — then we are not writing.

Don't be fooled.

Getting Ideas Begins with Pre-Writing

You may have heard the expression that "writing is a process." The process is made up of several different kinds of activities.

Pre-writing is one of the activities in the process. While the writing itself — the formation of outlines, sentences, and paragraphs — is a constructural activity, pre-writing is a conceptual activity.

Pre-Writing Makes the Project Go Faster

Pre-writing allows you to gather thoughts, sort through raw material, organize ideas, and eliminate rabbit trails. Decisions you make during pre-writing give you a sense of direction allowing you to get from Point A (a devotional to be written) to Point B (a completed devotional) in the shortest route possible.

Pre-Writing Gives Focus

It lets you avoid one of the stumbling blocks to clear writing: muddy messaging.

Pre-Writing Produces Authenticity

When writing devotional content, pre-writing offers one other indispensable component: it allows you to **uncover truth**. When it comes to writing devotionals, this is the most important facet of pre-writing — indeed, it may be the crux of writing sticky devos versus devos with less impact.

Think about Habakkuk. He didn't just wake up one day and decide to write down ideas that would eventually "make the cut" and be included in God's Word.

Habakkuk himself had a pre-writing process, even though he

may not have known it. He observed what was happening to his nation and his people. He took note of the physical destruction around him ... injustice in the courts and the rule of law brought to a standstill ... wicked people outnumbering the righteous.

Then he processed those observations. He wrestled to understand God's movement in what was happening.

Only after observing and processing did God tell Habakkuk to write.

A similar pre-writing process works for you and me.

- You get ideas by observation.
- You capture ideas.
- You process ideas so you're ready to write about them.

Stickable writers know that pre-writing is the key to producing quality work. The time spent here is essential for writing devotionals that stick because it is rooted in authenticity.

The process starts with getting ideas.

Getting Ideas: It's a Mindset

"Ideas are all around you."

I heard that statement a lot when I first started writing. It both encouraged me and intimidated me.

It encouraged me because it was comforting. If ideas are all around everyone, that means ideas are all around me, too.

But I was intimidated. Just because ideas were all around me did not mean that I could grasp them.

God understands that tension! That's why He gave us a very helpful message in Revelation 1:19: "Write down what you have seen" (NLT).

He didn't say write down what another writer has seen. He

didn't say write down what Hollywood celebrities have seen (unless you are a Hollywood celebrity) or write down what your pastor has seen. He didn't say write down what your mom has seen or your spouse has seen.

He said to write down what YOU have seen. (If you want to be technical, Jesus was telling the Apostle John to write down the revelation shown to him while he was in exile. But as with other scriptural principles, the concept applies to us, too.)

"Why me?" you may ask. "Who am I to write down the truth God revealed so that another person can read it?"

Why NOT you?

Through the ages, God has used ordinary people as His mouthpiece and in His work. Gideon, who considered himself to be among the least influential family in the least-effective tribe, led Israel to victory over a numerically superior Midianite army. David, the youngest of 8 brothers, became the king of a nation. Mary, a poor peasant teenager, gave birth to the Savior of mankind and raised Him to adulthood.

You are qualified because you have a unique perspective and because your observations are one-of-a-kind.

Do you feel unqualified? Good. To be a stickable writer, you need to be willing to obey God's call to "write down what you have seen" no matter how unqualified you feel about it.

But what if you feel qualified? Perhaps you're a mature Christ-follower or a leader with considerable experience. Maybe you have a special ministry call on your life.

If that is you, may I suggest that you check those "I'm - totally - qualified - because - I - am - a - leader" thoughts at the door.

An established platform can be a humility-killer and we all know how squelched humility morphs into pride. Pride is a big-time enemy of stickability. You don't want pride to stand in the way of God's movement. A platform may appear to boost your qualifications to write God's revelation and make it plain. Don't let this happen.

Figure out a way to dump the pride so you can get back to the business of looking at God's movement from your God-given unique perspective.

Do you want to be a stickable writer? Then adopt this mindset: ideas are all around you. Look for them.

If you don't think you see ideas, you can develop the ability to do so when you use the following simple set of tools.

Getting Ideas with the 6Ws: A Simple Tool to Use

Imagine all kinds of words, images, and conversations fluttering around in the air — and that you are able to capture them and make them understandable.

That's what an antenna does.

An antenna receives signals from a transmitting mobile device, radio, or television station and then translates those signals into data that people can use. (Technically-minded readers know there are more details to the process, which we don't need to get into here.)

When "the receiving antenna is up," it is ready to accept information from incoming senders, like telephone callers or radio waves or a news broadcast. The antenna receives the data and processes it so you can watch television programs or read text messages or listen to music.

When "the receiving antenna is down," it cannot receive signals. Transmissions are sent but they don't get through because the antenna is not able to fulfill its important role: processing the signal. That means your phone doesn't have service, you cannot find the radio station, or your television screen displays an irritating static screen.

The antenna is the go-between that connects the transmitting signal and the end user.

When it comes to getting ideas for devotionals, you are the antenna — the go-between.

Just as telephones and radio stations and television programs regularly send out transmitting signals, God regularly sends out signals, too.

Are you receiving them? You want to make sure those signals can get through. You get ideas for devotionals by making sure your writer's antenna is "up."

If this doesn't come naturally to you, it is a skill you can cultivate. If you are already a "natural antenna," you can become an even better one.

Make a decision to be an antenna and receive the signals God continually sends to you. You can do so when you train yourself to notice things throughout your day. There is a simple way to "put up your writer's antenna": use the 6Ws.

The 6 Ws

These questions are basic to information gathering, used by journalists to researchers to law enforcement officials to elementary school students.

And by devotional writers, too.

As you go about your daily business and a situation captures your attention, take a second to ask yourself these questions:

Who?

What?

Where?

When?

Why?

Wherefore?

OR PUT ANOTHER WAY ...

> Who did it?
>
> What happened?
>
> Where did it happen?
>
> When did it happen?
>
> Why did it happen?
>
> Wherefore did it happen? ... or How did it happen?

What Do You See — Literally and Figuratively?

Your antenna is up. You're observing events around you. But make sure you do so with both your physical senses and your heart.

Look again at Revelation 1:19: "Write down what you have seen." The verb "see" means to see both literally and figuratively.

You see literally with your physical eyes and your other senses — what you hear with your ears, taste with your mouth, smell with your nose, and touch with your skin — gathering information about people, objects, and circumstances.

You see figuratively by using the rest of your being, including your feelings, thoughts, and understanding.

Your combined "sight," both literal and figurative, gives you a pool of information about a particular topic. Writers have a word for this perspective: it's called your "point of view" (or POV).

By writing devotionals from your point of view, you share an observation from a particular angle — yours. You observe both literally and figuratively, with both your physical abilities and your intuitive abilities. What you see in a particular event or set of circumstances is unique to you.

Your distinct way of observing is a gift from God.

Observation: What Do You See from Your Point of View?

Let's look at an example — a short incident I'll call "The Runaway Shopping Cart" — from different POVs (points of view).

POV #1: You arrived at the grocery store (Where) before lunch (When), get out, and lock your car. Now you head into the grocery store to do your shopping (What). You hear a commotion and turn around to see a shopping cart (What) shooting across the parking lot (Where).

POV #2: After completing your grocery shopping (When), you load your groceries into the trunk of your car (What) in the parking lot (Where). A shopping cart whizzes by you (What). You hear an elderly woman (Who) scream, "No!" (What)

POV #3: You're in your car (Where) looking for a parking place (What) in a crowded parking lot (Where) when from the corner of your eye you see a shopping cart whiz by (What). You slam on the brakes (What) just in time (When). An elderly woman (Who) charges after the cart (What).

POV #4: You're a security agent on duty (When), employed by the grocery store. As you observe the camera feeds (When, What) from the parking lot (Where), you see a man (Who) opening the back door of an older model car (What). Suddenly, a wayward shopping cart (What) is headed directly towards him.

Write Down What You Have Seen

Why should YOU be the person to write a devotional about a runaway shopping cart?

You Have a Unique Point of View

Different points of view offer different spiritual lessons, even when rooted in the same incident. Why else would God include different versions of the same story in different gospels?

As for the Runaway Shopping Cart incident, even if each of these four individuals writes about this episode, each devotional will be different.

You Observed

You've taken to heart the truth that "ideas are all around you," and in the process of working to cultivate your observation skills, you happen to take note of the runaway shopping cart. Others in the scenario have other priorities (which is fine, by the way — not everyone is called to write devotionals.) Maybe the college student loading groceries into the trunk of his car saw that the elderly woman was safe and took off to his next class, never thinking another minute about the incident. He had other concerns at the moment.

You're Ready To Find the "Why"

Notice that these observations address Who, What, Where, and When. But to find the "Why" and the "Wherefore" ("So What?"), you need more information.

You learned something. Perhaps the hurried driver slammed on his brakes, cussed under his breath at the elderly woman, and found a parking spot as far away from her as he could. But you stopped on your way into the grocery store, noticed an elderly woman and her flying grocery cart, and thought of a scripture verse ...

And it's become YOUR story.

It becomes a devotional when you use it to illustrate a truth from God's Word.

Write it down. Write down what you have seen.

One Myth about Observation

When I first started getting serious about writing devotionals, I made a decision to work at being more observant. But I believed a myth.

I mistakenly thought that good ideas always must come from big events. In order to write an effective devotional, I thought I needed the "Big Reveal" — such as being witness to a dramatic conversion experience, a sensational rescue, a dramatic healing, or an overwhelming transition.

It's not that powerful stories like these don't produce powerful devotionals. They can. But the truth is that some of the most profound ideas often come from the most ordinary circumstances.

Don't gloss over your daily experiences. Observe them ... and then see what God shows you through them.

Try This

For the next 24 hours, try an experiment. Make a conscious decision to use the 6Ws throughout your day. To give you a start, I've listed places to look in Appendix A: Where to Look for Ideas.

You have a better chance of seeing what God wants to show you when you regularly ask questions and gather information from the answers.

Once you decide to be intentional, you'll start to notice things you didn't notice before. When you notice things, ask God to show you what they mean.

He will.

Because you're becoming more stickable.

5

HOW STICKABLE WRITERS CAPTURE IDEAS

My hand is on the gasoline pump waiting for my tank to fill when I see two other drivers jockeying for position in line at the opposite pump. Their fingers tap on their respective steering wheels, but neither one sees that two pumps are free on the other side of the central kiosk.

If they'd just turn and look in another direction to see what's there, I think.

A seed idea for a devotional forms. That scenario is a lot like how I get blind to opportunities from God. I get so focused on my first thought that I don't see God opening up other possibilities.

It's a seed idea that needs to be developed, but an idea nonetheless.

I'll remember that, I think.

But I have learned that I won't ... unless I capture the thought.

Capturing Ideas: It's Part of the Pre-Writing Process

Your mind continually receives thousands of tiny messages. Some are sensory messages. Others are informational messages.

Researchers tell us that our brains handle tens of millions of sensory signals on autopilot every second, such as light sensors allowing you to see details in a digital photo of your grand-daughter or olfactory sensors that allow you to distinguish between the different smells in the mall food court. Your brain is able to identify sensory signals from different senses and then categorize them to prevent sensory overload.

But information overload is another matter. It is a modern trend birthed in print material that has now mushroomed in the digital age to nearly unlimited information access. Your brain has limited short-term storage. Too many inputs shut it down. TMI ("Too Much Information") is not just a warning to flash to friends when they share ultra-personal life details. Information overload is a cultural phenomenon.

Add one additional element to the information tsunami: your intentional decision to observe life around you.

All of the sudden, you're not only bombarded with too much information, too many choices, and too much multi-tasking to process and sort, but you're also seeing indications of God everywhere.

Can you say "deluge"?

Enter in a crucial step in pre-writing: capturing your ideas.

You haven't truly adopted the "ideas-are-everywhere" mindset until you figure out a way to capture the ones that come your way.

You need to find a way to remember them.

KATHY WIDENHOUSE

Capturing Ideas: A System Is the Solution

You need a system — a way to record or organize the ideas God gives you.

Capturing ideas is obedience in action

Let's put practicality aside for a moment to focus on the spiritual: when you have a system to capture your ideas, you do more than just record a fleeting thought.

You also free your mind from worry that you'll forget that thought. In seeking to be obedient to God to "guard what has been entrusted to you" (1 Timothy 6:20), capturing ideas indicates faithfulness in the small things.

He has entrusted an idea to you. In turn, you capture it to ponder at the right time.

Capturing an idea reinforces it

As I take notes, an idea is underlined in my mind. The physical act of recording the thought adds emphasis. Reinforcement heightens awareness and I become more aware or more sensitive to other examples of that principle.

Capturing ideas gives you raw material

As you capture thoughts, you develop a pool of information from which to work. You don't need to process ideas right after capturing them. Keep them to sort through later (more about that in the next section).

The point is for you to have a system to take notes or record ideas as God gives them to you. That way, when you sit down to write a devotional, you don't need to start writing from scratch.

Recently as I sat down to write a weekly devotional for a client, I glanced at the clock. I had one hour to produce the content.

I did not know what I was going to write.

But I had notes.

I was in the middle of a 4-part devotional series based on one scripture verse. During the time that I initially mapped out the series, I had studied the verse in several different Bible versions. I wrestled with how different renderings translated one particular verb. I studied the meaning of the word in the original Greek, looked at related passages, and took notes. I captured my ideas!

That study time opened up four different slants on the same verse. Each slant was unique.

So when it came time to write the four devotionals, I had context for a series. I had raw material from the four different translations and ideas about how to communicate a separate concept from each one. All I had to do was write.

Incidentally, the notes were on a dog-eared, teacup-stained sheet of legal paper.

It was a system. And it worked.

If you capture ideas, you'll find you will process your ideas eventually — when the time is right.

Capturing Ideas: Try Different Systems

Writers use all kinds of different ways to capture their ideas.

It doesn't matter **how** you capture ideas. What matters is that you **do**. Here are few of the ways writers keep track of the ideas that come to them. Experiment with different approaches to find what works for you.

Capture Ideas In Your Journal

If you regularly process thoughts or jot down ideas that God is speaking to you in a journal, then you also know to review those notes every few days to look for patterns.

As you review, look for ideas for devotionals.

Make note of them. Pay particular attention to interesting twists that relate to events in your life. You can even create a special code or use colored pens or pencils to note devotional ideas.

And if you don't journal yet, consider starting.

Capture Ideas In Your Bible

Write in it. Underline scriptures and make notes of ideas in the margins. Record dates. Jot down related references.

Don't stop at just your print Bible, but take advantage of your mobile device and download a Bible application — one that allows you to take notes.

You'll find the app to be indispensable when you get an idea during a worship service or when you're listening to the radio, hear a speaker, and get a thought you want to remember.

Capture Ideas During Worship

During your personal study in the Word, God will give you ideas — a thought-provoking idea about a particular passage ... a "Eureka!" moment in which you see something new in a familiar story ... a unique way of combining two references to a similar principle. Even messages you hear on the radio podcasts can move you to take notes on the back of a napkin and process them for later. God regularly speaks through worship songs and lyrics. Does one particular phrase stick in your mind? What is the concept and how does it speak to God's movement in your life? If you don't have a place in which you keep your notes during worship — whether corporate or individual worship — then find one. You'll need it.

After years of struggle with knowing how to take notes during personal and corporate worship, I now have two systems. The first is a stack of index cards. I take notes during Sunday messages and then file the cards according to key scriptures referenced. But when it comes to my personal Bible study, I organize my notes in a 3-ring binder according to topic or book of the Bible.

Capture Ideas On Your Phone

A thought comes to you while you're in the car, sitting in traffic, or whizzing down the highway. Other times you snap a picture of a news item you see while reading a magazine in the doctor's office or record an audio message for yourself on your phone while you're working in the kitchen — all with the intent to process the information later. Yes, there is an app for that! Use a note-taking smartphone application (Evernote or Catch All, for instance) to help you collect and organize your ideas.

Capture Ideas On Paper

Keep a small notepad beside your bed, in your handbag, in your pocket, at your desk, or all of them. Jot down notes as they come to you on a scrap of paper — yes, even on a napkin in the restaurant. Just make sure you save it and file it.

Capture Ideas In Files

Hard copies or computer file folders — go with whatever works best for you or use both!

One advantage of having physical file folders is that you can save magazine articles, flyers, junk mail, or another other piece of paper in folders labeled by topic.

Computer files offer other advantages: convenience (you can access content with just a click) and back up (you can access them remotely when you back up your files to the Cloud.)

One Myth About Capturing Ideas

When I first got serious about writing, one of the pieces of advice I heard over and over was this: "Carry a notepad to record ideas as they come to you."

So for years I kept a small notepad in my handbag. Every six months as I changed out handbags for the summer season to winter or vice versa, I looked at the notebook. It became progressively ragged. Once in a while I flipped through the notepad, tore out the ripped pages, tossed them, and slipped the notepad back into my handbag. There it remained until about six months had passed again.

But I didn't use the notepad (except to record the occasional phone number.) To me, using the notepad would be an immense chore. I would need to dig through the handbag, find the notepad, fish around for a pencil, and write down the idea. By that point, I was so frustrated that I'd forgotten my observation or how I connected the idea to God's Word.

Finally, I ditched the notepad. It didn't work for me. I found lots of other ways to capture ideas, including those listed above.

The myth: good writers capture ideas in a notebook.

The truth: good writers capture ideas. You simply need to find out the best ways to capture yours. (It may be a notebook or it may not.)

Capturing Ideas: Find Your System

It doesn't matter which system you use. What matters is that you use a system or more than one.

Which system do I use?

All of them. Some I use more than others.

If you don't have a system in place to capture ideas, then get started. Choose one or two of the ideas above and see how they work. Or create another process that fits your lifestyle. But do something.

If you already have a way of capturing devotional ideas, then you need to know if your system is working for you. Ask yourself these questions:

- Do I purposefully use my system?
- When I go back and look at the thoughts I've captured, am I regularly surprised at what I see (because I would not have remembered the idea otherwise)?
- Do I use ideas from my system to write devotionals?

If you answer an unequivocal "yes" to all of those questions, then bravo!

If not, then make some changes in your system so you can capture ideas for devotionals and use them.

Because what's the point in having a system if you don't use it?

If you are serious about writing devotionals, you need to find a way to capture the ideas God gives you.

Capture the idea — and then you'll be in a terrific position to process it.

6

HOW STICKABLE WRITERS PROCESS IDEAS

Once you start getting ideas for devotionals by observing life around you and capturing those thoughts, you need to connect the dots between what you see and how God shows Himself in what you see.

It is this connection — putting the two together — that helps make a devotional sticky.

You need to process what God gives you before you start writing about it.

Process Ideas: Listen

That's what happened with Samuel as a boy. He had to process **what he was hearing** in order to understand **how God was in** what he was hearing.

Samuel had been sent to live with Eli, the high priest, to train to serve in the temple. One night, Samuel heard a voice calling to him. He mistook the voice for Eli, never thinking that it might be God. So Samuel went to Eli. And not just once, but three times!

Eli explained that God was calling out to Samuel in the

night. The next time God spoke, Eli said, Samuel should respond by saying, "Speak, for your servant hears" (1 Samuel 3:10).

Samuel did — and was able to hear God's voice directing him. He went on to become one of Israel's great prophets.

What exactly happened here?

Samuel's antenna was up. He was being observant. His openness allowed the information to get in and he captured God calling his name. Eli pointed him to God and told him to listen.

Once he knew that God was trying to get his attention, Samuel was able to hear what God wanted to say to him.

You face a similar situation in processing ideas for devotionals. Once you put up your "writer's antenna" and begin to intentionally observe people and events all around you by using the 6Ws, you begin to acquire a significant amount of insightful information.

Then you connect the dots.

You may immediately recognize the "God connection" in those experiences. Or in the moment, you may not. You may simply think "that's a cool illustration" or "I need to remember that" or the idea takes a special hold in your mind or heart and you capture it for further thought. Later, you sort through that idea to understand the "God connection."

Eli didn't connect the dots for Samuel. He helped Samuel **know how** to connect the dots. When he heard the voice, Samuel was to respond by saying, "Speak, Lord, I am listening."

That approach works for us, too.

As you review an idea, bring it before God and ask Him to show you any connection that He wants you to see. Say to God, "Speak, Lord, I am listening. Does this observation show me something about You — and if so, what do you want me to see?"

You invite God to direct the process of sorting.

That approach helps open the door for God to guide you,

point you to ideas He has for you, eliminate others, and pursue and tag some to process further.

And I know you'll agree that God's direction is a wonderful thing.

Process Ideas: Sort

"Processing ideas" is another way of saying that you sort through ideas and determine which ones to discard, which ones to hold to pursue at another time, and which ones to process right away.

I like to compare the sorting process to a traffic light. It's a familiar word picture that is often used to help people understand God's leading.

A typical traffic light has a red light ("Stop"), yellow light ("Caution" or "Wait"), and a green light ("Go").

A "red light" answer from God means "No," at least for now.

A "yellow light" answer from God means "Wait. Proceed with caution."

A "green light" answer from God means "Yes!"

This principle applies to processing ideas for devotionals, too. As you invite God to review ideas with you by saying to Him, "Speak, Lord, I'm listening," He will help you sort them by giving you signals. Those signals go something like this ...

Red Light

"No. Don't pursue this idea." In some cases, God says no because the idea or your approach is not scriptural. In other instances, the illustration may be too far of a stretch for a memorable devotional or it is a clichéd approach to a well-worn topic. Perhaps the topic and the idea is spot on, but you are not to be the one to write about it. A red light signal does not mean that you are not to write devotionals. It simply means that you are not to pursue writing a devotional about that particular idea.

Yellow Light

"Wait. Proceed with caution." Maybe you're not ready to write a devo about a particular idea because you need to learn more about how to apply the principle yourself. Perhaps writing the devo now might hurt someone close to you. Maybe God wants you to invest your time and energy on another topic right now and come back to this concept in a month. Perhaps God will give you more information to supplement this idea later on. "Wait" does not mean "No." It means the timing isn't right.

Green Light

"Go. Pursue this idea and write about it!" A green light means it is time to wrestle for the connection.

As you bring ideas before God, how do you know what traffic signal you're getting? We'll discuss ways to discern sticky devotional ideas in Chapter 11.

One Myth About Traffic Signals

Like me, you've sat at seemingly unending traffic lights, grinding your teeth in frustration while pounding the wheel. Why does the time appear to drag? Because I want the light to change according to *my* schedule.

Transfer that principle to God's traffic signals. When I pray, "Speak, Lord, I am listening," am I giving Him lip service? Perhaps I pray that prayer to "check it off my list" but in reality, I want to pursue my own agenda.

If so, then I may mistakenly pursue red light or yellow light ideas. Those ideas won't be sticky.

God's revelation is not on any particular timetable. In other words, His traffic signal — the connection between an observation and a biblical truth — may come quickly, in the form of an "Ah ha!" moment.

Or you may find yourself pondering a situation for an hour or a day or week or even months. Perhaps the observation continues to percolate in your mind, weaving in and out over a season of your life, until you understand the biblical truth and make the connection to the illustration. There may be times where you make a compelling observation but do not understand how it is connected to a biblical truth until you dig deeper into the scriptures yourself.

God places you in situations He wants you to notice so that you can write about them. In fact, He entrusts those experiences to you.

When you say, "Speak, Lord, I am listening" and truly seek His signals, He will give you a red, yellow, or green light. The green light ideas are the stickiest because they are given to you on God's timetable and pass the muster of readiness.

When it comes to being a stickable writer, make sure you bring your captured ideas to God and let Him do the sorting with you. Sorting with God saves time, aggravation, and prevents you from writing dull devos.

It also helps you grow.

Process Ideas One Dot at a Time

Remember that Eli, the high priest, did not connect the dots for Samuel. Rather, he helped Samuel identify God's call as a "dot" that he needed to connect.

Processing ideas for devotionals is like connecting the dots. You need to identify the "dots."

A devotional is made up of three key elements: a biblical truth, an illustration, and a takeaway. (In Chapters 13 - 15 we'll discuss each of those structural elements in depth.)

Think of each of these three elements as "dots."

As you sort through ideas, you'll notice that they are different kinds of "dots." Some are biblical principles. Some are illustrations. Some are takeaways. As you process ideas, you examine each one to understand what kind of "dot" it is. Is it a scriptural principle ... an illustration ... or a takeaway?

Let's look at an example.

As you sit down to sort through the ideas you have captured, you're listening to God. Three ideas leap out at you.

Idea #1: You happen across this passage during your Bible reading: "You shall be like a watered garden" (Isaiah 58:11). As an enthusiastic home gardener, the passage attracts your attention. You capture it by making note of it and think about it that afternoon as you water the cucumbers.

Idea #2: During your vacation, your vegetable garden's irrigation system developed a leak. When you return, you see that one area of the garden had been watered plentifully. Another had been cut off from the water source. The contrast is striking and you record the observation (after you water the dry section of your garden.)

Idea #3: You've been careful to protect your personal daily time with God by developing consistency in your Bible reading and prayer life. But this past week you experienced an unsettling disquiet when you heard an announcement during your church service, inviting volunteers to participate in a particular project. You jot a quick journal entry about your restlessness.

Think of these ideas as "dots" in a dot-to-dot puzzle. What kinds of dots are each of them?

Clearly, Idea #1 is a biblical principle. You've got a specific scriptural reference. On top of that, the verse resonates thematically as a scriptural theme: the Bible uses the image of water elsewhere to indicate literal and metaphorical sustenance. Idea #1 clearly alludes to the powerful spiritual truth that a spiritually-nurtured soul is a healthy soul.

And what an amazing illustration in Idea #2! It's got vivid details and a brief story line with a beginning ("I set my water timer and went on vacation"), middle ("The irrigation system leaked and only part of the garden got water") and end ("Part of the garden was healthy; part of the garden was shriveled.")

Idea #3 is a little trickier. It's not a scriptural principle ... it's not technically an illustration. Rather, you record a nudge in your spirit — an action to take — to examine your life and your choices.

A sticky devotional connects the dots between those three elements. Just like a "dot-to-dot" worksheet in a children's activity book, you use words to link together those "dots" so they form a circle. As a stickable writer, you develop the ability to connect those dots.

We'll connect the dots of these three ideas in a minute.

Which Comes First: The Scripture, the Illustration, or the Takeaway?

Do you get all three ideas at once? Sometimes.

But more often, you capture ideas one dot at a time. That's why processing is so helpful.

The good news is that you can use any idea as a launching point for writing a devotional.

This may come as a surprise to you because many people mistakenly think that getting ideas for devotionals is predictably linear.

That is, you may think that you should get an idea for a scripture, an illustration to go with it, come up with a takeaway and BOOM! You write the devotional. Done. Next.

Sometimes it happens that way.

But often, getting ideas is more circular than that. To understand further, let's ask this question. Which came first — the chicken or the egg?

If the chicken came first and then laid the egg, how did the chicken get here?

If the egg came first and then hatched into a chicken, how did the egg get here?

I ask the question not to goad an argument about creationism versus intelligent design versus evolution. Rather, I ask in order to point out the age-old issue of circular thinking ... and how circular thinking applies to getting ideas for devotionals.

Writing devotionals raises the "chicken-or-the-egg" question. As you process the ideas God has given you, which do you zoom in on first — the scripture, the illustration, or even the takeaway? If you knew which one to write first, you can just follow that formula, right? Especially when you're learning to write such a specialized genre.

News flash: ideas for any of the three can come first.

If the idea for the scriptural principle comes first...

You study a scripture and get inspired to write a devotional.

As you ponder it, God shows you an anecdote, fact, quote, or unique piece of trivia to illustrate it.

But maybe God inspires you with an illustration ...

You ponder the illustration and as you do, God shows you a scripture. The illustration reflects scripture's truth beautifully.

Or perhaps you've learned an important life lesson ...

As you process the lesson, God takes you backward through different sets of circumstances and scriptures that have helped you experience transformation.

Sticky Ideas Are Circular

We humans like to think sequentially. We tend to think that the creative process is linear: you get an idea. You write about it. You edit it. You submit it or publish it. Then you start the process all over with another devotional.

But the process of writing a devotional is more of a circle than a line. You can jump into a circle at any point — at any "dot" in the dot-to-dot sequence.

Perhaps you jump on at 1 o'clock on the circle (with a scripture) ... or between 3 o'clock and 9 o'clock (in the body) ... or at 11 o'clock (at the takeaway.) As long as you keep going around the circle, you can eventually complete the devotional.

Let's go back to our example.

Scenario #1: The idea for scripture comes to you first.

You process the idea you got from your Bible reading: "You shall be like a watered garden" (Isaiah 58:11). What a vivid word picture! You jump right onto the devotional dot-to-dot circle between 12 o'clock and 1 o'clock with this one and you can't wait to write about it. Your eye drifts out your back window to your vegetable plot. What kind of watering schedule do you use? What steps would you take to water your garden while you were on vacation? What happens when you don't water or water too much?

Scenario #2: The illustration idea comes to you first.

You process the irrigation leak scenario. The area of the garden that had been thoroughly watered now boasts a bumper crop of green beans. But on the other side of the plot, the tomato plants are shriveled up. You jump onto the devotional dot-to-dot circle between 3 o'clock and 9 o'clock to figure out how this incident illustrates a spiritual truth.

Scenario #3: The takeaway idea comes to you first.

You're careful to nurture your personal time with God, but the challenge to serve doesn't come so naturally to you. In other words, that area of your life doesn't get much "water." When you're challenged to volunteer, you squirm. As you ponder your disquiet about serving, you gaze out the back door and notice your Garden-of-Eden vs. desert vegetable plot. It looks a lot like your walk with God: one area is flourishing, while the other is withering. Some areas of your life get "watered" (your personal time with God) while other areas shrivel up (service.) But God wants your entire garden to be healthy.

Where Should You Start Writing?

Which comes first: the chicken or the egg? Or when it comes to writing a devotional, should you start with the scripture, the illustration, or the takeaway?

Like a dot-to-dot circle, the process of getting ideas for a devotional doesn't always have one clear starting point.

Start with the dots God gives you. When you get a "green light" idea, just jump into the circle. And keep writing until you've made it all the way around.

One Myth About Processing Ideas

When I first started writing devotionals, I had a misconception about getting ideas. If I was a writer, I reasoned, then ideas would be obvious to me. "Sticky ideas will hit me over the head," I thought.

Not always.

Sometimes an observation will connect immediately with a

biblical insight. But more often than not, I have to think about what I've observed and ask God to help me make the connection. The process drives me to the Word and to my knees in order to zero in on a biblical principle.

As you observe circumstances around you and ask, "What does this show me about You, Lord?" you discover that you are growing. Which is a great place to be.

Devotional ideas that are authentic — that show how *you* made the connection to God's truths — are the ones that stick.

Try This

"Speak, Lord. I'm listening. What do you want me to see? " Ask this one question. Do your part to observe and to capture your thoughts. God will help you connect the dots.

PART 2: STICKABLE READERS

———

7

STICKABILITY — IT'S ABOUT YOUR READER (NOT YOU)

Pastor Fred slammed his fist on the oak lectern, startling me. Others sitting nearby jumped, too.

"Do you hear that?" he asked, pounding his fist once again. He paused. The church was silent. Then Fred tapped gently on the stand. "What about this?" he whispered. "Yes, it is a knock, too. Can you hear it?"

My pastor was referring to Revelation 3:20: "Behold, I stand at the door and knock." He used an object lesson with different kinds of knocks — aggressive and gentle, loud and subtle — to demonstrate how God reaches out and speaks to us in different ways.

Fred had my attention. During that season of life, both my husband and I worked full-time while raising our two young children. My days were busy and noisy. I was ready to get some answers about hearing God in the midst of a chaotic life.

I was stickable.

I gained a powerful takeaway that day: God could speak to me, even during upheaval. I needed to listen in a variety of ways so I could hear Him. Now, years later, I regularly ask myself, "Is

God knocking at my heart right now? Is He asking me to listen so I can hear Him speak, even if it is in a way I have not heard Him before?"

Pastor Fred's demonstration has remained with me. I don't remember the exact date I heard that message. I don't remember the rest of the sermon. But I remember that one biblical principle and I remember the illustration. It has stuck with me as I have applied it in my daily walk, shaping the way I listen for God's movement in my life.

A devotional sticks when it grabs a reader's attention. Do you know what grabs your readers?

Stickability: It's About Your Reader (Not You)

Let's turn to our friend Habakkuk, who faced the same challenge that we do: sharing a particular message with a specific segment of readers. Habakkuk had received special insight from God. He also had a mandate to share that insight in writing with the people.

"Write the vision; make it plain on tablets, so he may run who reads it" (Habakkuk 2:2).

It can be tempting to read just that first part of the verse and the beautiful call we writers get from God — to "write the vision (and) make it plain on tablets."

But oops ... there's more to the verse.

"Write the vision; make it plain on tablets, *so he may run who reads it*" (Habakkuk 2:2, italics mine).

The process of writing down the vision was not for Habakkuk's benefit. It was for his readers' benefit — "so he may run who reads it." Habakkuk was to record what he received from God and then package it in a way that the reader could read it and then take it with him in his life's journey.

In other words, the purpose of writing devotionals is to benefit the reader.

That's not to say that you will not profit from the process. That you are a beneficiary in the process is a key point of this book. Indeed, when you are a stickable writer, you will grow, too (as we discussed in the last chapter), because sticky devotionals grow out of your growth. In fact, I'd argue that if you don't grow as a result of writing devotionals, then perhaps you can become more stickable.

Habakkuk processed the "green light" truth he had received from God and presented it in a way that his audience could receive it.

The content you present, the slant, the mechanics, the language ... all of it **starts** with you, but it's not **about** you. It's about the reader. It is to be constructed so that it directly benefits the reader.

Two Stickability Factors

Think back to The Tape Principle in Chapter 2, which explained that the writer and the reader need to be stickable and the devotional content needs to be sticky in order for there to be a connection.

When it comes to being a stickable writer who creates sticky devotional content, there is much you can control. You can take action to become more sensitive to God's leading. You can write and rewrite content so that it is sticky.

But when it comes to a reader's stickability, you have significantly less sway. For instance, you cannot control a reader's heart, making it more pliable and open to truth. You can pray for that to be the case, but cultivating a receptive heart is the job of the Holy Spirit and the choices made by the reader.

You can, however, impact two stickablilty factors in your reader — both having to do with getting her attention.

Stickability Factor #1: Know Your Reader

A reader is stickable when the content gets her attention and resonates with her. If you know who you're writing to, then you'll frame content to relate to her. Pastor Fred's knocking illustration stuck with me because I desperately needed to find ways to hear God in my noisy, busy life. It was relevant.

You help increase your reader's stickability when you write in a way that is relevant to her.

Simply put: know your reader and her needs.

Stickability Factor #2: Know Where Your Reader Reads

A reader is stickable when the devotional content is placed in his path. A devotional that is handy and convenient to him captures his attention. If you know how to get your devotional into your reader's hands, then he can read it.

Bottom line: Is the devotional accessible to your reader?

Make sure you do everything you can to get traction with these two stickability factors so your readers can read your content and run with it.

The next two sections will help.

8

STICKABILITY: KNOW YOUR READER

"I'm pregnant."

Think of the different ways a woman might deliver that information to another person.

- She might do so in a hushed voice of awe to her husband after five years of trying to start a family.
- She might do so in conciliatory tones when delivering the news to her shocked, house-bound, elderly parents.
- She might do so with confidence and authority as a high-powered executive to her board of directors, explaining why she must take a leave of absence during a crucial merger.

The news stays the same, but the woman reports it differently to different people.

Don't you?

How you present information depends on your audience.

Think about this pregnant woman. She knows enough about

these different people to know how to speak to each of them so they can best receive what she says.

For instance, her husband has yearned to start a family. When she tells him she is pregnant, she shares the wonder of a shared dream come true.

The woman's parents, however, are in poor health. They rely on her to help them in the home and with their personal affairs. She presents her news to them as an opportunity for them to extend the family line, quietly acknowledging to herself that they might possibly resent this turn of events.

At work, this woman manages a significant budget, operations, and a good-sized staff. Her board will be anxious about the impact of her news on the company's earnings, so she tells them she is pregnant by presenting a clear strategic plan outlining interim leadership roles and steps for her staff to take during her maternity leave.

This woman speaks in a tailored way to each audience. She frames the same piece of information with a specific slant customized for the listener so they can receive it.

She knows her listeners and what makes them stickable.

You can do the same as you write devotionals.

Know Your Reader's Three Big-Picture Needs

You do not know who will read your devotionals, but you know a few things about them.

Look at how our pregnant woman approached her board of directors. She may have been acquainted with a few of them, but she didn't have an intimate relationship with any. She merely understood generalities about them.

You know from your own life that the same is true for readers, particularly when it comes to spiritual issues. Each of us is in a different place in our relationship with God. Needs vary from person to person. No matter how insightful you may be, you cannot know specifics, let alone a comprehensive scope of each of your reader's detailed daily spiritual needs. Nor can you know how her needs may change from day to day.

Plus, there are simply too many readers, too many needs, and too many complex issues for you to speak to them all. (If you doubt this, then think of the waves of movement in your own day-to-day walk of faith.)

However, you *can* know some big-picture needs about your reader ... and then keep those generalities front and center as you write.

This is especially key when writing devotionals because this form is so structured.

Remember that a devotional is a short, inspiring illustration with a biblical takeaway. So your reader — no matter who she is or where he is in his life's journey — needs **short, inspiring, relevant** content.

Meeting those three big-picture needs makes content stick-able. Let's look at each one.

Need #1: Your Reader Needs Brevity

Habakkuk's message to the people was brief: invasion was coming as a judgement against God's people for their rebellion. (God also told Habakkuk that the invaders would eventually face justice, too. See Habakkuk 1-2).

The message was short and to the point. Brief as it was, the message may not have included specifics. (When would the invasion happen? Who would be attacked first?) Nevertheless, God was giving the people an opportunity to hear the truth and respond.

The truth can be brief or lengthy, but it is still the truth.

Given the upheaval permeating Judah at the time, a short message was efficient and practical.

A short message gave each person the chance to process the information and respond — and even the chance to get out of Dodge (or should I say Judah) if they chose.

When it comes to the need for brevity, today's readers are not too different from the people in Habakkuk's time.

Brevity Is Sticky

People in Habakkuk's time were distracted by their circumstances and their lifestyle. Political maneuvers and military coups swirled about them. Meanwhile, many were busy being wicked.

Like them, people are distracted today, too. We're busy. We live in a noisy world.

Whether or not people are too busy or need to be busy at all is a debate for another day and another book. The fact is that our lives are very full with jobs, families, activities, travel, and technology. Today's lifestyle — at least in western cultures — is fast-paced.

The speed of life and deluge of choices work to isolate us and distract us. Our lives are fractured as we move quickly from activity to activity, group to group. We have little time to build relationships of depth and seemingly less to wait on God.

Christ-followers know they need time with God and His Word. They think about God. They pray (often on the fly.) They go to church. They may even be a part of a small group or Bible study. They want to fit in more time with God. And they need a way to do it.

Our busyness and distraction makes our hearts stickable.

That's one reason why using devotional books and online devotionals has become so widespread. Devotionals are brief. You can read one in five minutes or less. A devotional wraps scripture, content, and a takeaway in a package that the time-deprived can use during their busy days. It offers truth in snapshot form, putting a spotlight on one phrase, verse, or short passage of the Word and gives the reader a smidgen of understanding about that passage.

That tiny bit of truth may not seem like much, but it is still truth. Devotionals offer a way for readers to read the Bible in tiny bits and pieces so that truth seeps into their lives. It is a tool that allows readers to have a snippet of time with God, in His word, in a way that is relevant to daily living.

I've heard pastors brush off devotionals as "Christianity Lite" because devotionals are short. Their length, the reasoning goes, means these pieces can play only an insignificant role in a person's walk of faith.

It's understandable that our leaders want more for their people than simplistic platitudes in a short reading.

But what about when a short piece introduces a biblical principle in a unique way ... when the piece challenges the reader to face a hard truth ... or even when the piece simply gives the reader pause to ask God for insight?

Much of walking with God happens in little moments throughout the day. As a reader goes about the business of life, a comment or a situation reminds her about a scripture or illustration or prayer from a devotional. The devotional taps into moment-by-moment living.

I'm not suggesting that a brief, 250-word devotional can take the place of an in-depth Bible study or daily personal time with God. But the beauty of a well-written devotional is its concise nature. Ultimately, God can use anything to reach us and grow us.

If your devotional has sticky content, your reader will use it. The key to effective brevity is quality.

In Chapter 12, we'll talk more about zeroing in on a specific, quality message in a devotional to maximize its impact. For now, know this: like the men of Issachar who "understood the times" (1 Chronicles 12:32, NIV), you can write devotionals as a way to share truth with Christ-followers in these times today, so readers who want to follow God minute-by-minute but lack extra minutes in their day can make a connection with God and begin to alleviate their isolation from Him.

Your job as a devotional writer is to communicate a biblical principle with brevity so that it sticks.

Bottom line: your reader can use short messages. He needs brevity.

Need #2: Your Reader Needs Inspiration

Struggle is nothing new. In the best of circumstances, life can be challenging. Jesus said as much: "In this world you will have trouble" (John 16:33, NIV).

You can bet there were people in Judah, like Habakkuk, who knew they were in trouble. They mourned the violence and degradation they experienced all around them.

Just as God's people of the past were looking into the face of trouble, today we look daily into the face of all kinds of trouble. Like them, we're hungry and thirsty for encouragement and wisdom and hope to process the volume of suffering and struggle we experience. And in today's times, bad news travels fast and with more frequency, often repeated over and over through different communications channels. We are hammered with it.

But there is more. The need for intentional inspiration is not only a response reaction to circumstances around us, but it is also a biological reality.

This need even has a name in scientific circles: negativity bias.

Negativity bias is the unconscious, default setting in your

brain that serves as a warning system, wiring you to accept negative input much more readily than positive input. Just one area of the brain (the left hemisphere) is assigned to process positive stimuli while two areas are devoted to negative stimuli (the right hemisphere and amygdala).

Two-thirds of the amygdala's neurons are dedicated to searching for negative experiences.

Meanwhile, it takes five to twenty seconds for positive input to even register in your brain, and it must be held there for more than 12 seconds in order to transfer from short-term memory to long-term memory.

Which means your brain unconsciously struggles to accept the exciting, positive, powerful truth of God's movement and activity.

That is all the more reason that every reader needs purposeful, authentic inspiration.

The need is not limited to just new believers or unbelievers who need encouragement. Even Christians who have been living a life of faith for years need regular doses of inspiration.

Heartache, discouragement, confusion, and our own default bias to negative thinking make our hearts stickable.

Inspiration is Sticky

In the face of negativity, devotionals offer inspiration in a digestible size. They are encouraging. It is another big reason why devotional books and daily online devotionals have become so widespread.

Sticky devotionals are **decidedly upbeat**. And why shouldn't they be? Our God is a God of new beginnings, exciting moves, and miracles big and small.

Plus, inspiration in devotionals is authentic. It is not a Pollyanna, just-think-positive-thoughts superficiality. Rather, true inspiration from devotionals stems from real life because it is written by real people who have experienced God firsthand. It is truth that generates hope that generates motivation, much like this:

Inspiration = Truth + Hope + Motivation

Inspiration allows the reader to see an exciting truth or a movement of God. That little beam of truth shines a ray of hope through the muck of adversity and confusion.

Hope motivates the reader to act.

The action can take many forms and vary in intensity, but is nevertheless part of the inspiration equation.

Reading short bits of inspiration from ordinary people people like you and me — gives hope and is motivating because it shows readers that God moves and is active through anyone.

You can frame inspiration in all kinds of ways. In Chapter 14, we'll talk about different kinds of illustrations you can use in devotionals to present truth in a way that imparts hope and motivates your readers.

But for now, know this: your readers need the different kinds of inspiration that devotionals offer. Inspiration prompts the reader to own the truth for herself. And who doesn't need that?

Bottom line: your readers need inspiration.

Need #3: Your Reader Needs Relevance

Did the people of Judah need to hear what Habakkuk had to say? Absolutely. Even if they were not jumping-up-and-down excited to learn that they were going to be invaded by the enemy, they most certainly needed to know that information in order to be prepared (if they chose) or make some changes in their lives (if they chose.) Once he gave them the information, the people would be able to take measures to act on it: to shore up their city walls, store food, build weapons ... or even repent and return to walking with God. Or not. What to do with the information was up to them.

But the information was relevant. The information that Habakkuk shared was directly applicable to their day-to-day world. They could put it to use. It was practical.

Practicality makes us stickable.

Today's readers are do-ers. They are busy, involved, and on-the-go. They want to put God's principles into action.

But here is where as a writer you need to know not just that your reader **should** take an action. Rather, **what** action can she take? And what kind of action resonates with this particular reader?

Think back to our pregnant woman. She shares a piece of information with three different audiences. Each one will have a different takeaway from the same piece of information.

- Her husband may respond by considering, "How does God want me to support my wife during this pregnancy?"
- Her parents may respond by asking, "How can we celebrate change rather than resist it?"
- Her board may respond by asking, "How can we execute an orderly, God-honoring transition?"

Clearly, different people respond to the same message in different ways, depending upon their circumstances and their frame of reference. Each takes away an application that is relevant to them.

The same is true with devotionals.

Relevance Is Sticky

Your devotional cannot be all things to all people.

A devotional, to be sticky, needs to target its readers. The language and presentation must be relevant to that audience. Think about it: a 6-year-old boy reads at a different level and with different understanding than does a 72-year old retired firefighter, who in turns reads and applies truth differently than does 30-year-old single mom.

God's truth can speak to each of them. In fact, the same biblical principle can speak to each of them. But how you present that truth differs from audience to audience.

You need to package the devotional principle so that your reader can receive it.

The best way to do that is to create a composite profile of your audience — the devotional's projected reader — and write to that individual personally.

It takes some research to understand your audience so you can write to them in a relevant way, but it's not hard.

You simply need to know a few questions to ask.

Try This

Create a Target Reader Profile

Start by picturing your ideal reader — the kind of person you imagine reading your devotional. Think of someone you know who fits your reader profile. Consider gender, age, worldview, experience, hobbies, interests, income, social position, purpose, and any other details that may be relevant. The more specific you can be, the better.

You can add or subtract elements from the reader profile to fit the devotional. For instance, perhaps you're writing a children's devotional that is suitable for both genders. In that case, your reader profile will not specify boy or girl. Or maybe you're writing a devotional targeting females who want to pursue a second career; in that case, interests matter more than marital status. Or your profile may contain more than one group of readers — fathers and sons, for instance. Include that piece of information as you brainstorm.

Use the checklist in Appendix B to help you create a reader profile. Then write to that reader.

Note that just because you write to a specific audience, you are not excluding others. People who do not fit your target profile will read your devotional and benefit from it.

Great!

Don't let that deter you from focusing your content to be relevant to a particular audience.

Bottom line: your reader needs content that is relevant to her — or at least content presented in a way that is relevant to her station in life.

Know Your Reader to Help Him Be Stickable

There you have it: three big-picture needs you can meet for your reader when you're writing a devotional.

Devotionals that are **short, inspiring**, and **relevant** — these are the kinds of devotionals that get your reader's attention. They make the reader more stickable.

Your reader becomes even more stickable when you place the devotion where he can read it so he can run with it.

Read on to learn how.

9

STICKABILITY: KNOW WHERE YOUR READER READS

You may have picked up this book because you want write devotionals to post on your personal blog. Or perhaps you have been asked to write devotionals for your organization, or maybe you need to present a devotional at a meeting. In any of these scenarios, you already have a specific, targeted audience: your blog readers, your organization's supporters, or the meeting's participants.

But maybe you have no idea yet who your readers will be. You're reading this book because you simply want to learn how to write devotionals (or write them better) and to find out how to get them in front of an audience.

No matter what your frame of reference, you can use this chapter to help you strategically and purposefully position your devotional for your target audience so that "he may run who reads it" (Habakkuk 2:2).

You need to make your content available.

Make the Information Available

In Bible times, there were no phones, no newspapers, no websites, and very, very few books or letters. Information was not readily available.

Further, scholars tell us that just 10% or less of the population in the ancient Holy Land could read and write. Word of mouth was the primary source of information sharing.

People interacted with others in their villages, but were isolated from other communities apart from when travelers passed through.

Information for public consumption was etched with an iron stylus onto tablets made of wood, stone, metal, or waxed surfaces. These tablets were hung on walls or set on tables in public places, in the temple, and even in homes — the ancient equivalents of newsprint, billboards, or the internet. This way, as many people as possible could be informed. The literate could read the announcements to those who could not read.

You can imagine that a new post would garner considerable attention, spreading its way through the community in a viral sweep.

That's what God told Habakkuk to do — make the revelation available to the people. He was to use the best means available at the time to reach the people he needed to reach.

There were limited means of sharing information back then.

But today, we have information overload.

In fact, mobility and connectivity have flooded our lives with input. "Too much information" is not just an idiom — it's a reality. These days it's not uncommon to feel you are drowning in information, whether it's coming from the web, text, social media, television, radio, other traditional media, or even conversation.

Even so, like those in Habakkuk's time, we too feel isolated. But it is not because we have limited access to information.

Rather, our isolation is rooted in the absence of community.

How ironic that we lack a sense of community in a time when we have more ways to communicate than ever before. People may be in physical proximity to each other but are not present with each other. If you doubt this, take a glance around any room and notice how many people have headphones tucked in their ears or mobile devices glued to their cheeks, preventing them from talking with each other.

That is one reason message boards, forums, and online communities spring up online. People hunger to connect with others. They do so in the ways that are available to them.

It's a reality you need to factor in as you write devotionals because it impacts your readers. They face the irony of feeling isolated while being connected to global information sources.

In order to connect with his audience, Habakkuk used the means at his disposal. You can follow his lead.

Today, you have multiple means available to you. You can position your devotionals so that they are in your reader's line of sight, allowing them to grab her attention.

Where are your readers reading?

Make It Available Today

These days, readers get content from multiple sources, or "channels."

In order to understand how to make your devotionals available to readers, you need to have a grasp of those channels. What are they? How do you post on them?

Once you know the different channels where your readers find content, you can consider and choose which ones will reach your target audience the best. Then you follow the trail to place your devotionals in those channels.

There is not enough room here to explain the publication

process in detail (nor is that the goal of this book), but a key part of the devotional writing process is understanding your reader so you can direct content to him. When you understand where your reader is reading, you can write accordingly.

A devotional's structure makes it well-suited for many channels. While other writing projects like articles or books take on a different form if they are destined for print versus online versus in person, a devotional's format stays largely the same regardless of the media in which it is produced. That means devos can be presented in more than one channel, largely as is. For instance, you may present devotionals at a staff meeting and then use the content to write blog posts. A few months down the road, you can repurpose 20 of those devotionals into a digital book.

Yet while a devotional's format is structured and suitable for multiple channels, the avenues to get a devo into publication differ from channel to channel. As you write, you need to understand those avenues so you can write specifically to a particular audience and for a particular channel.

There are two elements to consider:

1. Media: the channels in which devotionals are published
2. Publisher: the person or team that does the publishing

Media: Four Kinds of Publication Channels

There are four general media in which you can publish or present devotionals:

Print publications include books, magazines, and handouts.

Print publications build your platform as a speaker, leader, or writer. It is the favored reading format for older readers.

You can choose print publication via a traditional publishing route, which requires a submission and publication process but frees you from marketing your work.

You can also pursue print publication as an indie (independent) author, which is a faster route but leaves much more responsibility in your lap (See more about traditional versus independent publishing in the Publishers section (below.)

Online publications include websites, blogs, online magazines.

You can publish online as a contributor, whether as a freelancer, guest poster, or staff writer, in which case you will need to study the publisher's guidelines and submit content for the editor's approval. Look for online rights as part of a publication contract. You can also publish online devotionals independently on a blog or website, either your organization's or your own personal site.

Digital publications are downloads to be read on a mobile device.

Digital publications allow you to publish devotionals and devotional collections suitable to be read digitally.

While online publications "live" online, digital publications are individually downloaded and stored on the consumer's device. Younger readers prefer this format (along with online formats). Many publishing houses include digital publication rights as part of a publication contract.

In-person presentations include verbal devotionals at meetings, Bible studies, and groups.

As you present your devotionals, you need to know the requirements for content and time constraints. You may also want to prepare a printed handout to share with listeners to allow the devotional's message to be even stickier.

Publishers: The Person or Team That Publishes

Today there are two main categories of publishers: traditional publishers and independent (indie) publishers. Each route has various spin-offs, too. You can choose one route to publication or both. Here is a brief snapshot of the options.

Traditional Publishing

These books, magazines, pamphlets, and articles are edited, produced, and distributed by a commercial publishing house in print and online. The writer's responsibility is to write. The publisher's responsibility is to edit, produce, and market the work.

In traditional publishing, it is customary for you submit a devotional, a query, or a proposal to an agent or editor. If the work is accepted for publication, you sign a contract with the publisher and work with them through edits, production, and launch. The traditional publishing route allows you to submit single devotionals, a set or series, or an entire book.

Writers often develop strong relationships with editors and publishers, which can lead to multiple contracts.

- Timeframe to publication: weeks (online) to 36 months
- Author expenses: $0
- Advantages: prestige, professional production, marketing, distribution
- Disadvantages: longer time to publication, low royalties, less creative freedom

Independent Publishing (also called Indie Publishing or Self-Publishing)

In the indie scenario, you take on the role of author-publisher. These books, magazines, pamphlets, and articles are written, edited, produced, and distributed online or in print by ... you!

You have full responsibility for the end product. That may mean working with an editor and designer (to make sure your book is structured and formatted professionally) and marketing your work to get it into readers' hands.

Within the self-publishing realm itself, you have different routes you can take including publishing with a subsidy house, publishing a print-on-demand book, publishing an e-book or digital product, or posting your devotional online.

Independent Publishing: Subsidy Publishing

These books, pamphlets, or articles are published under the name of publishing house but at the expense of the writer. Quality, services, and costs range widely among subsidy publishing houses. Some simply produce an initial print run from your uploaded file. Other companies offer a range of design, editing, distribution, and marketing services for both print and digital production. In the case of devotionals, a subsidy publishing format is best for a book or collection, since individual devos are so short that you can print them from your desktop.

- Timeframe to publication: usually 90 days or more
- Author expenses: up to five figures
- Advantages: creative freedom, faster time to publication, global market
- Disadvantages: cost, less prestige, reliance on a production team, self-marketing

Independent Publishing: Print-On-Demand (POD)

Like subsidy publishing, this option is best suited to books and pamphlets (rather than single devotionals), which are printed and shipped when they are ordered by the consumer, hence the "on demand" moniker. As a writer, you don't need to run an entire printing at once, although you can order a short run for yourself. A number of companies provide print-on-demand services, including editing, design, and distribution services. (See Appendix C for a list of POD providers.)

- Time frame from completed manuscript to publication: as little as 24 hours
- Author expenses: $0 (do-it-yourself) and up (averaging $1,500 for professional services)
- Advantages: creative freedom, faster time to publication, global market, higher royalty share
- Disadvantages: less prestige, expenses, reliance on a production team (or do-it-yourself learning curve), self-marketing

Independent Publishing: E-Books and Other Digital Downloads

These works are formatted for a tablet, Kindle, iPad, cell phone, or as a download on a computer or electronic device. You can publish do-it-yourself, digital book or pamphlet downloads using software (Scrivener or Vellum, for instance) or publish in retail e-book stores. If you're not a do-it-yourselfer, you can pay a fee to full-service e-book publishing companies to format your manuscript into an electronic format. (See the Appendix for a list of digital publishing companies.)

If you're publishing just one devotional (or only a handful), you can print it as a saved PDF and give readers a special link to download it. This is a popular option to use as a freebie when you, your church, or your organization want to capture email addresses for an email list.

- Timeframe from completed manuscript to publication: 24 hours and up
- Author expenses: $0 (do-it-yourself) and up (averaging $1,500 for professional services)
- Advantages: creative freedom, faster time to publication, global market, higher royalty share, low risk
- Disadvantages: less prestige, reliance on a production team (or do-it-yourself learning curve), self-marketing

Independent Publishing: Web

A blog or website can serve as a platform for publishing devotionals. These online homes may be an organizational website, church website, or personal blog. The obvious benefit to web channel is immediate publication.

- Timeframe from completed manuscript to publication: immediately
- Writer expenses: $0 (apart from website or blog fees)
- Advantages: creative freedom, fastest time to publication, global market, low risk
- Disadvantage: less prestige, self-marketing, digital learning curve

Make It Available To Your Readers

If you're new to writing, all this talk of publication may feel over-whelming.

Don't let it be.

There are terrific resources available to you to market your devotionals to traditional publishers and to equip you to go the self-publishing route. The process has clear steps. People do it every day — people like you and me.

Right now, all you need to do is take one step in that process. That step is this: know where your readers are reading. That way, you can write your devotional to that audience, in a format that best reaches them.

Try This

Habakkuk knew how to best reach his readers. Do you?

1. Study your reader profile.
2. Choose a channel — just one at first. (You can add more later.) How can you best reach your readers where they read?
3. Choose a publishing route — just one at first. (You can pursue more later.) What publishing route can best meet your readers where they read?

It is about them. Make your devotional plain and easy for them to find ... so that he may run who reads it.

PART 3: STICKY CONTENT

———

10

STICKY CONTENT IS STRUCTURED

When I got serious about writing, I read everything I could get my hands on. Since I was interested in the faith-based niche, I specifically sought out books and articles that explained how to write devotionals.

Most focused on mechanics — the arrangement of the devotional and how to format each part in order to have a strong structure.

This makes sense. Devotionals are a specialized genre, so I needed to understand how to write them according to the accepted structure.

A well-organized format makes a stronger devotional. Once you know how to structure a devotional, the reasoning goes, then you can plug in the content.

There is a caveat: even the most organized, mechanically well-oiled devotional cannot make much of an impact without meaningful subject matter. You need sticky content.

Of course, sticky content begins with a stickable writer who understands his reader's stickability. But we've covered that.

So let's talk about sticky content.

Sticky Tape

Think back to The Tape Principle.

The scrap of paper and the refrigerator door are stickable — like the devotional writer and the devotional reader are stickable. The piece of tape, on the other hand, is sticky. It attaches to both the paper and the fridge.

The devotional is that piece of tape.

Dig into your desk drawer and find a roll of tape. Tear off a piece. Notice that one side of the tape is smooth plastic, paper, or fabric. The other side is coated with an adhesive compound.

The tape's surface — the plastic (or paper or fabric) — provides the tape's structure. The adhesive lets the tape attach to other surfaces.

The tape's surface and its adhesive are a unit that works together.

A devotional's structure and content, like tape's surface and its adhesive, are a unit that works together, too.

The structure is like the surface of the tape. It provides a way to deliver the content.

The content, like the tape's adhesive, makes the connection to the reader. (We'll talk more about content in the next chapter.)

Both structure and content go hand-in-hand to create a devotional that sticks.

The Sticky 3-Part Structure

Devotionals follow a standard 3-part structure: they include a scripture, an illustration, and a takeaway.

This structure is nearly universal in devotional writing. It's easy to understand why when you remember what a devotional is — a short, inspiring illustration with a biblical takeaway.

Each of the three elements has a special function.

1. The scripture

This short passage from the Bible forms the basis for the devotional and communicates a principle that is reinforced elsewhere in scripture, too.

2. The illustration

Sometimes called the body, the narrative, or even the "devotional" itself, this section explains the principle from the scripture by connecting it to an authentic life situation.

3. The takeaway

This part of the devotional, sometimes referred to as the "application," gives the reader a thought to ponder, a prayer to pray, or an action step to take in order to apply the devotional's scriptural principle. The takeaway describes to the reader how she will change in her everyday living if she takes to heart the biblical truth connected to the illustration.

Within this prescribed arrangement you can follow different formats. For instance, the three parts can be visually separated and even labeled, or they can flow together in one piece.

Some devotionals have extra elements, which we discuss in Chapter 16.

No matter how the devotional is presented or what additional elements tag along for the ride, the three essentials are present.

Why the 3-Part Structure Is Sticky

Why does this structure prevail in devotionals?

The 3-Part Structure Is Simple

You've likely heard of "The Rule of Three," in which the triad is a cornerstone structure for written material. In middle school language arts, for instance, you were taught to write a three-point essay. Pastors present biblical teaching in a standard 3-point sermon outline. "The Rule of Three" principle is demonstrated throughout time and across diverse storytelling genres from "The Three Little Pigs" to "The Three Musketeers."

All with good reason: the human mind is proficient at processing information in patterns. Three is the smallest number by which we can organize information in our minds. Ergo, The Rule of Three works in novels, essays, oral presentations, web pages, stories, letters ... and devotionals.

The 3-part structure makes a devotional stick.

The 3-Part Structure is Short

A devotional is a short form. By short, I mean devotionals are generally 150-500 words long. On average, a devotional's total word count clocks in at 200-250 words.

Its unique length sets it apart from other writing forms. There are plenty of reasons why brevity is sticky — including its appeal to busy readers, as we have already discussed.

But the brief length also means clarity. In an increasingly complex world, readers crave straightforward simplicity. When a short devotional presents truth clearly, it sticks.

The 3-Part Structure Is Practical

What better way to structure teaching than to present the principle, an example of how it has been lived out, and then a way to apply it? The order simply makes sense.

Plus, it's practical. A biblical truth plus an illustration lead to a tangible way to use the truth in everyday life. The concrete outcome appeals to today's readers, who are doers.

Formula Does Not Mean Formulaic

We will dive into each of the three elements to learn how you can write each one to be as sticky as possible. And we will use a very simple approach which you'll read about in the next chapter.

For now, know that the 3 -part structure gives you a formula to follow.

I can hear some protests now (in fact, I've made them myself): "If I use a formula, am I cheating?" or "Why follow a formula ... doesn't that limit the Holy Spirit?"

On the surface, using a formula may seem counterintuitive to writing a unique message in a unique voice.

But the fact is that a formula is simply a plan or an arrangement. A writer demonstrates creativity by being able to write engagingly within a formula's parameters.

And consider this: formulas have been around for so long because they work. If you don't use a formula, you could be in danger of misunderstanding how a piece is best structured to appeal to readers — a pitfall for many a writer. What may be misconstrued as a mechanical tactic can actually provide a proven framework to make your point and present it more strongly.

So when it comes to writing devotionals, the 3-part format is the way to go.

Using a formula does not mean a devotional is formulaic. This is an important distinction.

A formulaic devo offers a stock, conventional, well-worn, or clichéd content. It won't stick.

But a devotional that uses the formula to convey a biblical truth in a simple, authentic, and memorable way — this is a devo that is sticky.

Let's look at an easy, nearly foolproof way to make it so.

11

STICKY CONTENT IS S-A-M

BOTH STRUCTURE AND CONTENT GO HAND-IN-HAND TO create a devotional that sticks.

When it comes to the mechanics of a devotional, writers over the decades have come up with a structure that works — the 3-Part Structure. Like we've discussed, this structural format represents the "surface" part of a piece of tape.

In his words to Habakkuk, God gave a few pointers about how to write content — the "adhesive" part of the devotional tape.

Remember the verse?

"Write the vision; make it plain on tablets, so he may run who reads it" (Habakkuk 2:2).

This is extremely valuable information. You can see how this passage reveals three qualities of sticky content: it is to be simple, authentic, and memorable. Together, these three qualities make a sort of blueprint to follow as you write content. They are easy to remember by following a simple acronym: S-A-M.

S: Simple

Habakkuk was to write plainly. His content was to be simple and to the point — not verbose and complex.

A: Authentic

Habakkuk was to write "the vision" — divine revelation. He was to share the truth God gave him, not his own agenda. In other words, the content was to be authentic rather than sugar-coated; truthful rather than dishonest; deep rather than superficial.

M: Memorable

Habakkuk was to write the vision so that readers could use it. The content was to be memorable so as to be practical.

Use the acronymn as a checklist as you write devotionals. Read on.

S-A-M: Simple, Authentic, Memorable

The S-A-M acronym is an easy, powerful guide you can use to write your devotional. We will refer to it as we dig into each of the three parts of a devotional and show you how to use it as a self-check.

For now, let's look at each piece of the acronym.

S: Simple

"Simple" means "easily understood" and "containing few parts."

No matter what the idea — be it straightforward or complicated — you are to make it plain. You are to zero in on one clear, pithy idea.

And "simple" is not the same as "simplistic." You can write about a complex principle in a simple way that is concise and to the point.

This is THE key element to writing successful devotionals. I call it the "One Point Rule."

The One Point Rule is simply this: **Focus the content of the devo on just one nugget of truth.**

Becoming aware of the One Point Rule is the central step to writing devotional content that sticks. I wish someone had written that rule years ago and then explained it to me. It could have saved me untold hours of aggravation and dozens of rejection letters.

In fact, following the One Point Rule is such an important skill that we'll devote an entire chapter to it right after this one.

Why It Matters

Why is focusing on one idea in a devotional so important?

Chief among reasons is that readers read devotionals *because* they are simple. Readers don't use devotionals for a comprehensive study of a book of the Bible or even a complete analysis of one verse. They just want one thought they can mull over during the day ... one thought that will give them a deeper understanding of God or that will help them put their faith into practice.

Then too, you simply don't have room for more than one point in a devotional. A short word count can't cover more than one point well. If you try, then the devo goes in two or three directions but never drives home a takeaway.

You don't need to explain everything about God or even one topic in a single devotional. In fact, you should *not* try to do so.

If you have that much to say about a topic, you should probably write an article about it. Or even a book. Or you could write a series of devotionals, and use each devotional to focus on one point about the topic.

Not only is the One Point Rule the most important concept in writing sticky devotionals, but it can be the most challenging.

In fact, following the One Point Rule is such an important skill that I've devoted an entire chapter to it.

But the good news is this: the more devotionals you write, the better you'll get at focusing in on one point.

You'll get all kinds of tips for doing so in the next chapter.

Bottom line: Sticky devotionals are simple. They follow the One Point Rule.

A: Authentic

You've experienced "holy talk" — the kind of sharing in Christian circles that skirts the real issues. If you believe even half of those around you, then most Christians never struggle with having meaningful time alone with God, reading the Bible, guarding their words, keeping a pure thought life, or loving a spouse unconditionally. And that doesn't even begin to address the bigger stuff like raising rebellious children or dealing with an addiction or losing a job or dealing with prickly relatives.

"Holy talkers" are often well meaning. In fact, when you use holy talk you might not even be aware that you are doing so. It is part of the cultural tendency to wear a mask or set up a screen to protect yourself. You may not tell a direct lie, but you may not spell out the reality, either. In the process, your discussions become flippant or superficial.

Take Habakkuk's record of God's revelation. If he was talking holy, he could have written something like this:

"Some guys with a bad rep are traveling around. You may want to pay attention."

That's true, but it's not the full story. While that version doesn't use insider, holy lingo, it isn't completely honest or forthcoming, either.

Take a look at how Habakkuk recorded God's words:

Look among the nations, and see;

wonder and be astounded.
For I am doing a work in your days
that you would not believe if told.
For behold, I am raising up the Chaldeans,
that bitter and hasty nation,
who march through the breadth of the earth,
to seize dwellings not their own.
(Habakkuk 1:5-6)

Habakkuk could have been less than fully authentic because he didn't want to be seen as an alarmist, a depressing person, or a wacko. Instead, he manned up and communicated the reality as given to him by God: "Heads up, Judah. You need to listen big time. You're going to be overwhelmed to the point at which you may not believe it until you see it. You're about to be invaded — no, crushed — by an evil, powerful nation who will seize your homes and all that you own. It's going to get more than ugly. It's going to be downright devastating."

See the difference? Habakkuk called a spade a spade. He wrote the vision God had given him.

Sticky devotionals address real-life situations authentically — head on, with the truth.

Why It Matters

Authenticity matters because it oozes credibility.

When you face a life change, are you willing to proceed if the reason for change is not based on the truth?

No, I'm not either.

Change is hard enough when it is based on reality.

In a devotional, you're challenging the reader to life change. To be motivated to change, the reader needs to know that the challenge to do so is credible and grounded in the truth.

That kind of authentic writing requires vulnerability.

Predictability ...artificiality ... posturing ... phoniness ... superficiality: they are big enemies of stickiness. While you might feel more comfortable dancing around the edges of the truth in order to protect yourself, the reality is that writing the truth reveals the power of God working in your life or a life you've observed.

Authenticity can be easy to cover up not just with content but with lingo, too. Your audience is predisposed to spiritual things, so you might be tempted to communicate with Christianese as a defense against self-revelation. Soon you're writing about the blood of the Lamb and being sanctified. You may think those terms are acceptable because they are "religious" and because others use them.

While those terms represent biblical truths, the language doesn't connect to the reader with authentic, practical reality. Authenticity says, "I'm feeling angry and frustrated inside because I lost my temper at my son when he couldn't find his backpack and I said hurtful things! I don't want to be that way! I want to get this cleared up — with God and with my son and with myself."

That language is the real and authentic version of "I need the blood of the Lamb and I need to be sanctified."

Sincerity and vulnerability are powerful ... which is why authenticity makes a devotional stick.

Bottom line: Sticky devotionals are authentic. They force you to be vulnerable.

M: Memorable

A devotional principle becomes memorable when the writer uses words and content to make "good connections" in the reader's brain.

Let me explain how you, the writer, can lay out those connections for your reader. To do so, I'll need to revert to tenth-grade biology for a moment, so hang in there with me.

Your brain is made up of special nerve cells called neurons that send out signals, telling your body to do things. These cells have long arms that snake out, creating tens of thousands of potential connections with other neurons as they, too, send out signals. Since there are a *lot* of neurons in your brain (about a billion of them), there is potential for mega-amounts of connections.

Neurons are not joined or attached to each other. Instead, there is space in between them — space that needs to be bridged by connection.

It is bridged by special connections called synapses. Synapses permit a neuron to pass a signal to another neuron so that the messages can get through to the other parts of your body. They are like a docking point for one neuron to connect with another neuron.

The connections made by the synapses can be strong or weak. The stronger the connection, the more memorable it is.

So it makes sense that you want to stimulate strong connections in your devos so that the content is memorable.

At the risk of oversimplification (brainiacs, please forgive me), what makes an experience memorable — memorable being what strengthens those connections — are at least three things: existing connections, sensory details, and emotions.

Existing connections are previous pathways in your brain. If you build on an existing connection, your reader will focus on what is added to what he already knows — to that pathway. The existing synapses in between neurons that process this information get strengthened.

But if your reader is learning something new, his brain focuses on processing it and building new connections in between neurons to understand it. That piece of information is not as memorable. For instance, it is easier to connect and build upon what a classical musician knows about Beethoven than it is to connect with her about programming in Java script. (This is a big reason to write to your audience, as we discussed in Chapter 8.)

When you write a devotional that references a familiar topic for your reader, you build on existing connections. Your content becomes more memorable. It's one reason Jesus used parables.

Sensory details describe what you see, hear, smell, taste, or touch. Details that appeal to the senses activate the neurons in your brain. When writing devotionals, try to use sensory details in order to activate more neurons. In fact, if you can use more than one set of sensory details — such as both the sense of sight and the sense of taste — then you'll increase the chances of forming additional or stronger connections. Your content becomes more memorable.

Emotions "turn up the volume" of your content. When you invoke emotions in an honest and judicious way, you help intensify the connections between your brain's neurons. Your content becomes more memorable.

An Example of How Memorable Connections Work

Let's look at a concrete example of how your brain builds memorable connections.

You order a chocolate milkshake at a new restaurant. And for the record, you've had plenty of chocolate milkshakes before. (The existing connection has been already made in your brain.)

When your server brings you the milkshake, you notice its unique presentation. There is real whipped cream swirled on top, sprinkled with rich, dark Belgian chocolate curls. Your visual synapses are getting uber-excited. As you take the first sip, you can be sure there are chocolate-flavor synapse connections firing in your brain. The taste is luxurious and rich. (Sensory details are vivid.)

Then you glance at your bill. The milkshake costs less than one you'd order at your favorite fast food restaurant! You're feeling some unexpected emotions right now, including pleasure to satisfaction to surprise. (Emotions intensify the experience.)

All kinds of neurons are firing in your brain. Existing connections create a point of comparison with other milkshakes you've tasted in the past. Sensory details bombard your neurons with a beautiful visual and delectable, rich chocolate taste. And you certainly have an emotional response — you're getting a great deal, but you certainly weren't expecting one!

That's how the brain makes memorable connections.

Sticky content follows those principles and makes memorable connections in the brain.

Bottom line: Sticky devotionals are memorable. They make connections through experience, the senses, and emotions.

Test S-A-M Stickiness

Let's put it all together and look at an example to see how S-A-M Stickiness works when you write devotional content — and how you can test your content against the formula.

On vacation at the shore, Cynthia found an unusual seashell on the beach. It was a perfectly-formed but fragile shell encased inside a larger, stronger one.

She saved it.

To Cynthia, the shell inside the shell was a visual representation of how she abides in Christ. She is small and fragile. But our Lord is strong. He surrounds her, covers her, and protects her — represented by the outer shell. She can abide in Him, just as the smaller, more vulnerable shell rested securely inside the protective, stronger, larger one.

Cynthia is Cynthia Heald, a well-respected Bible teacher and speaker. She used the seashell illustration as a centerpiece of her 31-day devotional book, *Abiding in Christ* (NavPress Publishing Group, 1995), which addresses a woman's steadfast relationship with Jesus from all kinds of angles.

I first read the shell-within-a-shell devotional years ago when a dear friend gave me the book as a gift. The illustration stayed with me.

Let's see how it measures up to S-A-M Stickiness.

S: Simple

The devotional is simple, clearly communicating the message from John 15:4-9: it provides an image of "abiding in Christ." Early on in my journey of faith, the concept of "abiding" seemed "religious" to me — even complicated. How could I "abide" with Someone I couldn't see? Once I read this devotional, it made more sense. The word picture helped me understand how I am encased by Christ.

A: Authentic

Because the devotional is honest and real, I have been able to apply it. I've called upon the image of a shell within a shell when pierced with the uncertainty of starting a new job. I acknowledged the protection of Christ's "outer shell" surrounding me when I became a new mother ... when I lost loved ones ... each time when we moved our children to college. I learned that one part of abiding in Jesus means letting Him protect me when I am vulnerable.

M: Memorable

While there are many other facets to abiding in Christ, the visual image of a delicate shell encased inside a stronger one has remained with me. Beach vacations gave me a reference point from which I could relate to shell hunting. As I read the devotional, I could hear the pounding of the surf and feel the gritty sand beneath my toes. But the word picture also evoked emotions, including courage and comfort.

Cynthia's devotional stuck to me. It is short, it is authentic, and it is memorable.

It's the kind of devotional you can write, too.

Try This

As you write your devotional, run it through your S-A-M test:
- Simple: what is my one point? Write it out.
- Authentic: is the content real? You know it is if you feel a bit vulnerable or exposed.
- Memorable: does the content stick in your mind — and why? Note existing connections, sensory details, and emotions.

12

STICKY CONTENT MAKES ONE POINT

STICKY DEVOTIONALS MAKE ONE POINT. THAT POINT illustrates a biblical truth.

Putting the One Point Rule into practice is ***the*** key skill you need to write devotionals that stick.

Sometimes as I begin to write a devotional, the point is evident. In fact, there have been times when the point comes to me as an idea. I capture the idea (Chapter 5), process the idea (Chapter 6), and then write about it.

But most of the time I have to sift through all the content I've gathered and work to find the point.

Pathways to One Point

As I process the content to "get to the point," I face one of three scenarios.

1. Too Many Points
2. Too Broad of a Point
3. No Point

The good news is that each of these pathways can lead you to identify one point for your devotional. With a bit of practice, you can learn to recognize these pathways and dig through quickly to get to your point.

Path #1: Too Many Points

The most common challenge we writers face in writing devotionals is that we try to make too many points in one piece.

This is the single biggest reason devotionals don't stick.

What happens is that you may have thorough content, but you sure don't have a short piece. There is too much information crammed into your draft. And thorough does not necessarily equate with inspiring.

And remember: a devotional is a short, inspiring illustration with a biblical takeaway (a Point.)

Every devotional idea can convey several points. Even the shortest scriptures or simplest illustrations offer more than one nugget of biblical truth. As you write, you need to be aware that the possibility exists for multiple points. But you need not — and should not — make every one of them in the piece.

Rather, your job as a devotional writer is to identify one point and drive it home.

Choose One Point

Read the Parable of the Lost Coin — short by any account, clocking in at just 3 verses (Luke 15:8-10). A woman loses one coin out of ten and searches diligently until she recovers it. Then she celebrates her find with friends.

Your devotional referencing the lost coin can speak to the value God places on each individual ... how God passionately pursues people who are lost to the Kingdom ... or the heavenly celebration that takes place when just one person enters the Kingdom. All three are valid points and this list is just a start. You can think of many more ideas to add to the jumble, I am sure.

You can see how there are many different directions a devotional's content can take — and they're all good.

Which one is the point of your devotional? If you end up hitting too many points — whether unintentionally or not — the devotional is too long and too confusing. It won't stick.

Write down the points. Then choose one.

I hear the push back now because I've used it so many times myself: "I've got the different points in my head."

To which I say this: if you have all those different points in your head, then it will only take a minute or two to jot them down. Do it.

Write. Down. The. Points.

You'll be amazed to find out how much clarity you get when you put things in black and white. Once you make a list of points, you'll be better able to identify one of them as the issue for this devotional and then purposefully target your writing to make that point.

Choose one. Write it down. Then write your devotional to target that point.

Spell Out The Point

You may have a related scenario. You may think, "This story has only one point."

Really?

To you, maybe, but not to the reader.

Most of us don't want to work too hard when we read. That is why as a writer you must take the reader by the hand and lead him directly to the point by telling him what it is.

Let's look at an example to help practice spelling out the point.

Maybe you're writing a devotional about forgiveness. A high school tennis coach was harsh with you, even to the point of viciousness. His attitude turned you off to the sport and to physical fitness. But when you get to college, a friend invites you to play tennis. You watch others in the group play and realize that you can compete well with them — perhaps even win. You agree to play one match. But when you serve the ball, you see and hear your coach speak negativity into your life ... and you miss the serve. You're conflicted inside. You want to play tennis, but you have a roadblock. You realize you need to forgive your coach (whom you never see any more) in order to move on.

It's obvious to you what this devotional is about.

Or is it? Which of these is The Point?

1. Timing. Don't wait when you feel God's call to forgive.
2. Cost. Un-forgiveness has a cost.
3. Initiative. You can forgive, even if the offender doesn't ask for forgiveness.
4. Response. One response to Christ's forgiveness is to forgive others.
5. Freedom. Forgiveness brings freedom.

They all work! But you haven't told your reader which one is The Point.

For your devotional to stick, you need to zero in on just one point, write it down, and spell it out to the reader in the devotional content.

Sticky Tip: Too many points? Write them down. Choose one. Then spell it out to your reader.

Extra Tip: You don't need to include your Point in the devotional, although you can — if it fits the narrative. But if you don't write the Point within the devotional itself, be sure to write it down somewhere: in your draft, in another file, on a piece of scrap paper, or wherever. This way, you can refer to your Point as you write. You can make sure that everything in your devotional lends itself to contributing to your Point.

Path #2: Too Broad of a Point

I sometimes take a different route when working to get to the crux of a devotional: I mistake a broader topic for a point. A topic is too big to cover well in a short piece.

You can recognize this problem in devotionals when the content is superficial, cliched, preachy, or impersonal. The language may be trite and the answers too pat. The alleged "point" is simply too wide-ranging to zoom in on in a devotional and have significant impact.

Let's go back to our example about the would-be tennis player. As you work on the devotional you identify the point as "forgiveness."

"Forgiveness" is a big topic. We've already listed several ideas to pursue in making our point. How can you drill down to one of them?

The best way is to test your ideas against scripture. Make sure you can identify each idea's roots in the Bible.

This is a terrific exercise to do to make sure you're on solid theological footing. Along the way, you'll learn more, too. You'll discover all kinds of details about your topic. And of course you'll find tremendous encouragement in seeing God's principles from the Word evidenced in your life.

By looking at the five ideas extracted from the draft devotional above, you can find scriptural evidence to support each one:

1. Timing. Don't wait when you feel God's call to forgive.

"Today, if you hear his voice, do not harden your hearts" (Psalm 95:7-8).

2. Cost. Un-forgiveness has a cost.

"In anger his master delivered him to the jailers until he should pay all his debt. So also my heavenly Father will do to every one of you, if you do not forgive your brother from your heart" (Matthew 18:34-35).

3. Initiative. You can forgive, even if the offender doesn't ask for forgiveness.

"Father, forgive them, for they know not what they do" (Luke 23:34).

4. Response. One response to Christ's forgiveness is to forgive others.

"Be kind to one another, tenderhearted, forgiving one another, as God in Christ forgave you" (Ephesians 4:32).

5. Freedom. Forgiveness brings freedom.

"For freedom Christ has set us free; stand firm therefore, and do not submit again to a yoke of slavery" (Galatians 5:1).

Each of our potential points has a strong biblical foundation. All support the theme of forgiveness as put forth in scripture. That's good news!

Further, each scripture addresses the topic from a different angle. Each addresses a particular biblical principle that explains the concept of forgiveness in a unique way.

Isn't that one of the amazing aspects of scripture — that each principle has so many facets? Taken separately, each point can stand alone. Taken together, different components of a topic give a more comprehensive understanding of that biblical principle.

Once you test various points against scripture, your task is to choose the biblical point the devotional should make. Is there a scale that makes one of these points more important than another? In other words, should you focus on the idea of forgiving others (Point #4) rather than the cost of not forgiving (Point #2) because forgiving others is "more Christ-like"?

No. Here is where I urge you to "not shrink from declaring … the whole counsel of God" (Acts 20:27). A devotional is a way to give your reader one step of understanding — one point — about a broader topic. Your point about forgiveness — the particular angle you address in your devotional — may be exactly the truth a reader needs. Which biblical point is best demonstrated by your illustration? Use it. Give yourself permission to write the answer God gives to you.

Likewise, give yourself permission to not cover ALL elements of the topic in each devotional (back to "Too Many Points.") You can get that permission by carefully choosing a scripture verse. The verse provides a nugget of truth that speaks to your point.

To make one point and write a devotional that sticks, know the difference between a broader topic — a biblical theme — and one facet of that theme.

Make your point from that one angle.

Sticky Tip: Too broad of a point? Test for the best. Test (against scripture) for the best (point.)

Path #3: No Point

A sticky devotional focuses on just one point. But what if you can't find a point in all the muck you've written down?

You may just have a good story or you may have a scripture verse stuck in your head. But you don't have a devotional … because you don't have a point.

The pathway to the point is by finding a connection. If there is a point to be had, then you can find the connection to it from your illustration or your scripture by asking a simple question.

Ask This Question

So what?

In other words, what difference does the illustration or the scripture make? Is there a conflict and resolution? Is there an object lesson?

If you have an illustration, then ask God to show you how it connects to the Word or a biblical truth.

If you have a verse, study it. Ask God to show you why He keeps persisting with bringing into your heart and mind. How does it connect to real life?

Or as the radio commentator Paul Harvey (1918-2009) would say, you need to know "the rest of the story."

Finish the Story

Most of the time when I struggle to identify a point, it is because I don't finish the story or finish the thought. I may have an illustration, complete with scene and conflict, but no conclusion. Or I may have a phrase from scripture that keeps niggling at my mind that begs an illustration, but I haven't pursued it as deeply as needed.

So I look at the scene or the scripture and ask, "So what? What difference does it make? What is the rest of the story?"

Let's dig deeper into our tennis player example.

Right now the third-person story doesn't reveal the rest of the story. What happened to the stunted athlete? Maybe she stepped off the court and called a good friend who prayed with her to forgive the coach. She was able to return to tennis and today plays twice a week. In this instance, she experienced how forgiveness brings freedom (Point #5).

The story may wrap up another way. Maybe the girl recalled all the times since high school that she avoided tennis. She changed channels when a tennis match was on television ... walked extra blocks around the college tennis courts so she wasn't tempted to watch practice... had surrendered the fun of being on her college club tennis team out of fear. Un-forgiveness had a cost. She missed enjoying her favorite sport. But today, on the court, she was confronted with her stubbornness. She couldn't wait any longer. She forgave the coach (Point #2).

In another scenario, the tennis player realized she had embraced a lie. She thought that her coach had to admit his wrong and apologize for her to be healed from the hurt. But as his angry face clicked onto the slide deck in her mind, she was startled. She hadn't seen her coach in two years. He lived three states away. He likely did not even remember his behavior towards her. If healing was to happen, she needed to take the initiative. She could forgive, even if he didn't ask for forgiveness. (Point #3)

What's the end of the story? Find it and you'll find your point. You may find several. (In which case you'll need to sift through too many points and choose one.)

Sticky Tip: No point? Finish the story.

Getting to the Point

There you have it. Your pathway to a short, inspiring point:

1. Too many points? List them (as in write them down.) Choose one.
2. Too broad of a point? Test (against scripture) for the best (point.)
3. No point? Finish the story.

There is no preferred route. None of these pathways to the point are better than the others and none are exclusive. Often, I take all three. They work together to provide checks and balances to show me that I truly am focusing on one point.

This is one instance — identifying the point of a devotional — in which the end justifies the means.

As long as you get to the point.

13

STICKY SCRIPTURE

Let's dig into how to write each element of a devotional.

Not long ago, I attended a special worship service at the invitation of my daughter. The speaker was a well-respected Bible teacher.

The passage he chose to speak on? Psalm 23, the beloved Shepherd's Psalm that opens with "The Lord is my shepherd, I shall not want."

I memorized Psalm 23 years ago. I have had my children memorize it. I have attended dozens of funerals in which Psalm 23 was the cornerstone passage.

Could anything said that evening be new, fresh, or have stuck?

God continues to surprise!

The speaker zeroed in on one tiny phrase inserted at the very tip of Psalm 23:3: "He leads me in paths of righteousness **for his name's sake**" (emphasis mine.)

Whereas much of what I have previously derived from this beloved passage has always been about the Shepherd's presence, comfort, and protection, now I had another insight. One reason God leads me to walk in His paths is for His reputation — for "his name's sake."

The speaker took a good deal of time to address the concept of reputation. As you can imagine, that topic resonated with the largely under-30 crowd. (And to be honest, the over-30 crowd, too.)

Then he tied the Christ follower's life to God's reputation. The paths that I walk and the ways that I choose to live my life impact God's name. He purposely leads me to walk in right standing with Him so that others might see Him ... "for his name's sake."

Guess what? I read Psalm 23 differently now.

"For his name's sake" sticks with me.

Choosing a Sticky Scripture

How do you choose a sticky scripture for a devotional?

First, a key point: all scripture is sticky. "All scripture is inspired by God and profitable for teaching, for reproof, for correction, and for training in righteousness" (2 Timothy 3:16, RSV).

But at issue here is not whether a scripture passage is sticky. They all are or can be, because God speaks through His word.

Rather, the issue is **choosing** one for your devotional.

Think back to our discussion in Chapter 6. As you process the ideas God has given you in order to write a devotional, you may zoom in on a scripture, an illustration, or even a takeaway. Any of the three may come to you first.

If the scripture comes to you first — or if you're assigned a scripture to write about — then choosing a verse for the basis of your devotional becomes a moot point. The choice has been made. (You'll face a different challenge when it comes to writing the illustration or the takeaway.)

But what if God speaks to you through an illustration or a takeaway?

Then you need to go about choosing a scripture that connects with the rest of the content.

This is a crucial step. Since a devotional is a short, inspiring illustration with a biblical takeaway, you want to be certain that the illustration and takeaway are grounded in a biblical truth.

The biblical principle is the foundation of the devotional.

In order to find that biblical truth, you may have to dig. But that may be the best outcome of all, because YOU will grow!

God can give you a truth through an illustration or takeaway or any other means, if He wants. Whether you receive the truth through an idea for an illustration, as a takeaway, or by pondering and studying, God's truth is still truth — no matter what path you take to get to it.

Choose a Scripture that Has Made You Grow

In my Psalm 23 experience, I had wrongly anticipated that I'd hear a well-trod version of "God is our comforter." And I had wrongly assumed I couldn't learn any new insights from a section of scripture I had known for decades.

But God used the familiarity of the passage to help me see a different biblical truth. A surprise insight made the message sticky.

Should you stay with familiar passages because they resonate with readers ... or should you choose less well-known passages in order to connect readers with a wider base of the truth?

The answer is "yes!" to both.

Many of us — writers and readers alike — are tempted to camp out in more comfortable parts of scripture.

No problem. Do so. And when you discover a unique insight, then share it in a devotional.

But don't be afraid to dig into less-trafficked territory in the scriptures. You will uncover riches. They are there. Otherwise, God would not include those passages in His Word.

In fact, you may be compelled to spend time in parts of God's Word that are less-familiar territory if an editor assigns you a set of devotionals to write from one of the minor prophets or if writer's guidelines specify, "We like to publish meditations based upon lesser-known portions of scripture."

The point is this: to choose a scripture for your devotional, get in the Word and be in the Word. Ask God to help you see the devotional's principle in scripture. Wrestle to understand it. Fight to find out how God speaks to that principle through you.

This may happen quickly or it may take some time. Let God do His work.

Then whether a passage is familiar or unfamiliar, you will be surprised by a point God makes to you. It is that fresh insight that is so sticky. When you grow, your readers grow.

Choose a Short Scripture

The most effective devotionals use a short scripture passage — usually 25 words or less. Any more than that will be too long. Longer passages can muddy the waters, making it difficult for you to extract the one point you're trying to make and difficult for the reader to make the connection.

The Psalm 23 speaker used just one phrase for an entire 45-minute message: "He leads me in paths of righteousness for his name's sake" (Psalm 23:3). Devotionals are shorter than a full-blown message. A brief scripture can suffice.

Choose a Scripture According to Context

One of the land mines in devotional writing is the danger of quoting a scripture out of context. In order for your devotional to be powerful, its scriptural basis must be faithful to the truth it communicates. Does it stand alone out of context and still convey biblical truth?

In a discussion group, one friend struggled with the concept of forgiveness. "But scripture says, 'Vengeance is mine,'" my friend said. "I have been hurt and I have the right to get my own back!"

Uh, oh.

It was then that the rest of the group gently pointed out the context of those words: "Vengeance is mine ... says the Lord" (Romans 12:19). For many years, this dear man had harbored resentment and bitterness, believing they were his personal right ... all because he had taken the scripture out of context.

If he had taken a few moments to read the entire passage, my friend would have discovered that the reference is to God's words delivered to the nation of Israel through Moses (Deuteronomy 32:35). The reference was placed smack in the middle of a passage that describes different ways a Christ-follower is to show genuine love, generosity, and hospitality — even when wronged — and leave vengeance up to God.

When writing your devotional, you don't want to lead another person astray. Misrepresenting God's truth can be dangerous (take a look at James 3:1 if you have doubt.) As you choose scripture for your devotional, simply make sure the verse accurately portrays the biblical truth in your illustration.

A good way to confirm that you're reading context accurately is to compare the principle to other places in scripture in which it is referenced. For instance, if my friend had done a simple Bible study on "vengeance," he would have quickly discovered other passages in scripture that refuted his claim of resentment towards those who had wronged him.

Choose a Translation

An effective devotional references the Bible translation upon which it is based.

There are a couple of reasons for choosing and indicating a translation for the scripture. In the most practical sense, a publisher must reference the translation's publishing house in order to comply with copyright law.

Further, consider your readers. A person who regularly uses the New International Version (NIV) may see your devotional based on a scripture used from the New Living Translation (NLT). The wording is different but it speaks to her in a new or different way. She may want to read the context or even the entire chapter. Yet without the reference to the NLT, she will head over to her trusty NIV. She won't see the same terms and will get confused.

By referencing the translation, you clear up that confusion. You lead the reader to a new insight and to a deeper study of scripture.

You'll help God's word stick.

When it comes to mechanics, indicate the translation according to the publisher's editorial directions. Some prefer the reference to follow the scripture in parentheses like this: John 3:16 (KJV). Others favor an in line reference, like this: John 3:16, ESV. Find out which your publisher prefers and then use it.

Try This

Always run your scripture through your S-A-M checklist:

- Is it short? Choose a scripture that is 25 words or less.
- Is it authentic? Check the context. Does the point you're making in the devotional line up with the truth presented in the scripture?
- Is it memorable? Think of my Psalm 23 experience. Scriptures are memorable when you make the connection for your reader to the scriptural truth.

14

STICKY ILLUSTRATIONS

A DEVOTIONAL'S ILLUSTRATION IS SOMETIMES CALLED THE body, the narrative, or even the "devotional" itself. A good illustration connects a real-life situation to a spiritual truth (your One Point.)

Jesus was the master at making a point using an illustration. His illustrations are accessible, clear, and easy-to-understand. They are real.

You can learn from Him how to do the same when you write devotionals!

Jesus didn't try to be more spiritual than the rest of us. He wanted us to "get it" — to "get" Him. So Jesus filled His illustrations with realistic events and authentic characters to help us understand spiritual truth.

He did so in different ways. Sometimes He simply called out a metaphor: "I am the vine" (John 15:5) or "I am the door" (John 10:9). Other times, Jesus gave a short word picture, as in comparing the Kingdom of Heaven to a net (Matthew 13:47-50). And still other times, He told a full-fledged story and provided a detailed explanation to His disciples in private (The Parable of the Sower, Mark 4). In just a bit, we will take a look at different types of illustrations Jesus used.

But for now, let's understand how an illustration works to drive home your One Point.

Paint a Picture, Then Connect the Dots

A devotional illustration paints a picture in words. It works like a verbal slide in a slide show or a still photo pulled from a video.

When you paint a picture for your reader with words, he calls an image to mind. "A picture is worth a thousand words" is a cliche, but it's true.

An image is concrete. In contrast, devotional content usually addresses an abstract principle. Think love, joy, peace, patience, steadfastness, goodness, mercy, forgiveness, grace ...

An image helps make an abstract principle become concrete for the reader. It makes the connection to a spiritual principle — to your One Point.

Let's take another look at Parable of The Lost Coin, which we first referenced in Chapter 12.

Jesus told the story of a woman who had ten coins, but lost one. She searched her house from top to bottom, cleaning and sweeping even by the light of a lamp, until she found the missing coin. Then she called together her friends to celebrate finding it (Luke 15:8-10).

It's a **real life situation** — one we can relate to even today. Most of us have misplaced a wallet or checkbook at some point, and have experienced the heart palpitations and sweaty hands that go with that experience. You empty desk drawers ... search under car seats ... empty all your pockets ... retrace your steps ... all to find the wayward item.

Once Jesus painted the picture for His listeners, He then made the connection to a spiritual principle — **the point**:

"There is joy before the angels of God over one sinner who repents" (v. 10). The point being God and heaven's residents celebrate passionately when you are found by Him.

The concept of "Rejoicing of angels in heaven" — on its own — is abstract. As you picture angels rejoicing, you may imagine lots of wing-flapping and halo-tossing, but since you haven't experienced that kind of gathering firsthand, it is hard to grasp.

On the other hand, finding lost money is much more relatable. You can identify with the woman's celebration because you understand the relief and joy you experience with finding your wallet. The illustration helps you feel and understand a smidgen of how God celebrates with His fellow residents of heaven when you're lost and then found.

By using a real life word picture, Jesus helps you connect your experience to a biblical principle — the One Point — so it sticks.

Real Life Situation + Principle = Sticky Illustration

How to Connect the Dots: Use Details

A picture may be worth a thousand words, but you can only choose two hundred or so of them to make your point in a devotional.

And here's another part of the conundrum: your well-chosen illustration by itself is not enough to complete your devotional. You need to spell out how your illustration connects to your One Point, too.

It's that connection between the details that makes a devotional sticky.

This is the step that surprises many devotional writers. We think we should be nuanced and allow the reader to "figure out the spiritual truth for himself."

Remember that readers don't want to work too hard. What's obvious to you may not be obvious to them.

Like we discussed in Chapter 6 (when Eli helped Samuel recognize God's voice), think of your illustration as the dots in a connect-the-dots puzzle. In a puzzle, the dots connect one by one in sequence to lead you through to a conclusion. Likewise, in a devotional you need to lead the reader step-by-step sequentially to connect him to the One Point — the conclusion.

News flash: this is not the time for subtlety. Writing a devotional is not like writing a literary masterpiece.

Look at how Jesus did it. In the Parable of The Lost Coin, Jesus painted this real life situation using vivid details: the woman swept the house (no small feat on dirt floors and without a vacuum cleaner or Swiffer.) Jesus said she searched diligently, meaning thoroughly and meticulously rather than carelessly. She didn't give up until she found the coin, meaning she invested considerable time. Those particulars — the details — become the basis for the point that God is totally ready to celebrate when we are found.

It is the details in your illustration that connect your reader to your One Point — the devotional's spiritual truth. Explain in plain language how the details in the illustration reveal something about God. You're not done until you make that connection for the reader.

And as a bonus, you'll recall that sensory details make the illustration memorable — the "M" in S-A-M!

There are two simple ways to make the connection for your reader.

1. Draw a parallel. Make a point to show how the illustration's details reveal a similarity to God or what you read in the Word.
2. Draw a contrast. Make a point to show how the

illustration's details reveal a dissimilarity to God or what you read in the Word.

Draw a Parallel: "This is Like What I Read in the Word!"

A devotional idea came to me as I sat on my screened porch late on a beautiful autumn afternoon and noticed how the leaves had turned colors. A breeze ruffled past, caressing my cheeks and rippling through the leaves, creating a kaleidoscope of different colors of gold. Then a huge gust caught the branches, whipping them up and over and around, showing the leaves' undersides of brown and green. Though I could not see the wind, its two different kinds of movement called to mind the movement of the Holy Spirit, described by Jesus in John 3:8: "The wind blows where it wishes, and you hear its sound, but you do not know where it comes from or where it goes. So it is with everyone who is born of the Spirit."

I thought of two family members — both Christ-followers — who had been gifted to respond differently during a family upheaval. Each approach had strengths. As I studied the trees, I was able to draw the parallel to the Holy Spirit. We cannot see how the wind moves. Nor can we see how the Holy Spirit moves in people to gift them with strengths. However, we can see the effect of the Holy Spirit through people as they reflect God's strengths. He reveals Himself as He chooses by reflecting His beauty and strength in different ways.

Notice the details. My observation of the wind moving in the trees was not enough to illustrate the movement of the Holy Spirit and have the devotional stick. Instead, I focused on how the movement of the wind revealed the leaves' different colors. One family member showed her colors the best when God pressed into her gently. The other responded well in the gusts of crisis. That is similar to how the Holy Spirit moves differently in people.

Bonus: those details appealed to my sense of touch (the breeze on my cheeks), sound (the wind's whispers and gusts through the branches), and sight (golds contrasting with browns and greens.)

Draw a Contrast: "This Is Different from What I Read in the Word!"

I once wrote a devotional about a friend who had a hard time believing in God's presence because she couldn't see Him with her eyes and touch Him with her hands.

I compared our contemporary limitations to faith with Rahab. Today we have scripture, the internet, churches, and other believers, yet sometimes that isn't "enough" for us. In contrast, all Rahab had to go on were stories of God's faithfulness that she had heard from travelers, yet she risked her life to help Hebrew spies escape (Joshua 2).

Notice how I used details to make my point.

I offered a list of faith-building tools that are available to us today. I compared those with the few details we know about Rahab's exposure to the Truth. Her choice to believe, based on the available evidence, is an inspiring contrast to the proof we require today.

And note what I left out.

I could have addressed my friend's stumbling block in more detail and used it as an object lesson to faith. I could have pulled out a quote about risk and compared it to the risks the Hebrew spies undertook in faith. I could have used the conversation between Rahab and the spies as a basis for trust between believers.

But I used contrasting details to make One Point: each generation has limitations to belief, but you can respond in faith using the means God gives you.

Kinds of Illustrations to Use

The most commonly-used devotional illustrations are personal stories, anecdotes, conversations, statistics, object lessons, interesting facts, pithy quotes, and questions.

And where, you might ask, did this list of types of illustrations come from?

Jesus.

Take a look at this list of the kinds of illustrations Jesus used and some examples of how He used them. You may be surprised at how natural it can be to use authentic illustrations from real life.

Personal Story

Jesus had a lot to say about Himself and His activities. So do we.

Personal stories remain one of the most effective vehicles for illustrations in devotionals — with good reason. They are personal. We can share them with authority.

Take a look at this powerful instance when Jesus describes His encounter with Abraham. Jesus identifies the patriarch by name (a detail), how the patriarch acted (a detail), and his emotions (a detail.) The Jewish leaders didn't believe Him, of course, but Jesus used His personal experience to make a point: He is eternal.

"'Your father Abraham rejoiced that he would see my day. He saw it and was glad.' The Jews said to him, 'You are not yet fifty years old, and have you seen Abraham?'Jesus said to them, 'Truly, truly, I say to you, before Abraham was, I am'" (John 8:56-58).

Anecdote

While a personal story is about you, an anecdote is a story about someone else.

We cannot be certain that Jesus's anecdotes (parables) were entirely fictional; there is evidence that shows they were rooted in truth. You can follow Jesus's example and draw upon hundreds of your observations and interactions with others as material for illustrations in devotionals. The key factor here is to provide details that you have gathered. Jesus told all kinds of stories about other people: a dejected father, a persistent widow, an unrighteous manager, a rich fool. He even foretold His own rejection and death at the hands of the Jewish leaders — and eventual birth of the New Testament church — in the story of the vineyard tenants who beat, abused, and killed the owner's servants and son.

"What will the owner of the vineyard do? He will come and destroy the tenants and give the vineyard to others" (Mark 12:9).

Conversation

Have you overheard a conversation or have you been part of one that sparked a way to communicate a biblical truth? Jesus did, too. Here is a scene in which he overheard religious leaders talking with His friends. Jesus used that conversation as the basis for making a point about spiritual need. People understand what it feels like to be sick and need a doctor. Jesus used that word picture to identify human needs. By specifying needs, Jesus helped listeners understand their need for Him.

"And the scribes of the Pharisees, when they saw that he was eating with sinners and tax collectors, said to his disciples,'Why does he eat with tax collectors and sinners?' And when Jesus heard it, he said to them, 'Those who are well have no need of a physician, but those who are sick. I came not to call the righteous, but sinners'" (Mark 2:16-17).

Numbers

Numbers, by their nature, are specific and detailed. You can use numbers and statistics to make a point. See how Jesus uses numbers to talk about how God knows the details about your life and mine.

"Even the hairs of your head are all numbered" (Luke 12:7).

Object Lesson

An object lesson is a visual or physical example of a truth.

Recall your delight as you pass fields of wildflowers in bloom along the highway. They bloom in abandon. It is a specific picture that is clear in your mind. Jesus explained God's overwhelming provision by comparing lush wildflowers in a field to His provision for people.

"Consider the lilies of the field, how they grow: they neither toil nor spin, yet I tell you, even Solomon in all his glory was not arrayed like one of these. But if God so clothes the grass of the field, which today is alive and tomorrow is thrown into the oven, will he not much more clothe you?" (Matthew 6:28-30).

Interesting Fact

You may find that a news story, interesting fact, or intriguing piece of information makes a connection to a spiritual truth in a way that captures your imagination.

The fascinating process of germination in seeds, for instance, is of particular interest to gardeners. Jesus placed that particular information front and center as a detailed illustration to explain the principle of surrender. When a wheat seed is surrendered to the earth, the grain itself dies and produces a plant. The plant in turn bears a larger wheat crop.

"Unless a grain of wheat falls into the earth and dies, it remains alone; but if it dies, it bears much fruit" (John 12:24).

Pithy Quote

A quotation can provide a powerful illustration of a scriptural truth, as Jesus demonstrates here in a reference to the law of retaliation quoted from Exodus 21.

"You have heard that it was said, 'An eye for an eye and a tooth for a tooth.' But I say to you, Do not resist the one who is evil. But if anyone slaps you on the right cheek, turn to him the other also" (Matthew 5:38-39).

Question

Jesus asked more questions than He answered — an excess of 300 questions in the gospels alone.

Questions make listeners (and readers) think. They are sticky.

Jesus' questions helped the listener see different facets of a situation and go beyond simply looking at life in black and white. A legal scholar asked Jesus, "Who is my neighbor?" Rather than answering the man's question directly, Jesus wanted him to think about different ways he perceives people. That's when Jesus launched into an illustration that we call the Parable of the Good Samaritan, listing three specific people in the process. Then Jesus concluded with a question.

"Which of these three, do you think, proved to be a neighbor to the man who fell among the robbers?" (Luke 10:29-37).

A Few More Tips About Illustrations

How Long Is a Sticky Illustration?

The scripture and the takeaway clock in at approximately 25 words each. That leaves 100-200 words for the illustration.

Use them wisely.

Use One Kind of Illustration Per Devo

The illustration represents the bulk of the devotional. You can use nearly limitless means to illustrate a biblical point. Even so, be sure to narrow your focus. Don't share a fascinating fact to make your point and then tack on an object lesson. Target one truth with one illustration.

One Illustration + One Principle May = More Than One Takeaway

The parables of Jesus show us that different people learn different truths from the same story.

A reader may gain the same truth that you intended to convey in your devotional. He may take away a different thought entirely, yet one sparked by your devotional — and one he needed for this season in his life. Or he may take away more than one truth.

Your job is to use the illustration God gives you to make a spiritual point as clearly as you can. Your reader will take away what he or she needs ... when your devotional is sticky.

Try This

Always run your illustration through your standard S-A-M checklist:

- S: Is it short? Does the illustration use just one object lesson, one scene, or center on just one fact? You can share many details, but you're looking at just one slide in the slide show.
- A: Is it authentic? Check your language and delivery. Are you coming alongside the reader and sharing as a peer? We alienate our audience when we're holier than they are. Vulnerability breathes authenticity.
- M: Is it memorable? Illustrations are memorable when you make the connection for your reader to the scriptural truth.

15

STICKY TAKEAWAYS

James 1:22 says, "Don't just listen to God's word. You must do what it says. Otherwise, you are only fooling yourselves" (NLT).

James cautions readers against passivity and complacency. We are to put what we learn into action — to "do" something.

That's a key outcome you strive for when you write devotionals. When your devotional propels the reader to action, you know that it sticks.

The devotional's takeaway, also called the "application," is the third element in the 3-part structure. It is the most practical of a devotional's three parts. The takeaway gives the reader something to "do," such as an action step she can take in order to apply the One Point.

The question is, "what action?"

Takeaways Are Simple

This is where you, the writer, come in. Your takeaway suggests to the reader an action step to take.

The action can be big or small. It can be obvious or subtle. Regardless, the overarching guideline to follow is this: write a simple takeaway.

The biggest danger in writing your takeaway is being too specific. A good takeaway does not assume the reader's circumstances.

I realize this sounds counterintuitive, especially since you have already invested considerable effort in writing the devotional by being specific and detailed while choosing a scripture, identifying an illustration, and connecting the two together.

But here is where this element of the devotional equation differs from the other two.

A sticky takeaway does not suggest a detailed course of action. It does not assume the reader's circumstances.

Good devotionals stick when the scripture and illustration focus on details, but the takeaway points to a spiritual principle.

Takeaways Focus on a Principle

The beauty of scripture is that it can and does apply to such a wide range of circumstances.

You demonstrate that versatility in your takeaway.

Let's say you're writing a devotional for women about developing a respectful relationship with their in-laws, based on the biblical story of Ruth. Ruth's mother-in-law, Naomi, had faced hard times and had become bitter, yet Ruth responded to Naomi with loving grace and generosity.

As you write, you feel a tug to challenge wives to be loving towards their in-laws. Yet you have no way of knowing what kinds of circumstances your readers face. Perhaps one has a loving relationship with their in-laws ... maybe with another, there is estrangement ... still another has experienced a deep hurt from her husband's abusive parents ...

You want to encourage your reader to take a step in her life that puts into practice the spiritual truth from the illustration, yet your takeaway must use language that is broad enough to apply to women who are in all different kinds of relationships with all kinds of in-laws.

You can do so when you focus on the spiritual principle, rather than a specific step.

Compare these two takeaways:

1. Take a page from Ruth's book and show love to your in-laws by moving with them to a foreign country.
2. How is God prompting you to adopt an attitude of grace towards your in-laws?

Takeaway #1 focuses on a specific step: moving to a foreign country. It may apply only to a very select few readers. And it is not scriptural in that God does not call each of us to move to a foreign country with our in-laws.

Takeaway #2 focuses on a principle: adopting an attitude of grace. It is scriptural in that God always seeks to help us grow in showing grace. Yet the takeaway is also applicable to every godly wife. It challenges each reader to bring her attitude to God for inspection, listen to His response, and then take one step to adopt a more godly attitude towards her in-laws.

The reader's personal application will spin out of her circumstances. As you write, be careful not to assume those circumstances.

If the reader already has a loving relationship with her in-laws, God may show her how to cultivate even more grace towards them, perhaps by looking for an opportunity to express her respect for how they raised their son. Or God may call her to adopt an attitude of grace by being the first to reach out in an estranged relationship. If she has experienced a deep hurt from her in-laws, God may lead her to show grace by taking steps to develop an attitude of forgiveness while still maintaining healthy boundaries.

You can write clear, simple takeaways when you focus on writing about a specific spiritual principle — your One Point — rather than a specific action step.

Takeaways Are S-A-M

You write a simple takeaway focused on a spiritual principle, you meet the other two S-A-M requirements (Is is Authentic? and Is It Memorable?) in one swoop.

A: Authentic

A simple takeaway that focuses on a spiritual principle (the One Point) over a specifically targeted action step makes a lot of sense. Is it realistic to challenge readers to take a specific step that may not be appropriate for them, such as to pull up stakes and move to a foreign country with their in-laws? In a very minute number of circumstances, perhaps. In 99.9% of other cases, no. But there is always an authentic need to grow in grace towards family members, even in the healthiest relationships. A simple takeaway that focuses on the principle of growing in grace towards family members is authentic.

M: Memorable

It's true that a challenge to move to a foreign country with your in-laws may be memorable. But the challenge to show grace also tweaks emotions such as conviction, inspiration, remorse, or surrender. It is personal. Relationships pull at our emotions — a key prompt for memorability.

Simple, clear takeaways that focus on a spiritual principle are also authentic, memorable ... and thus, sticky.

Writing a Takeaway

Use a Template

If you aren't sure how to go about writing this element, try using a writing template to construct your takeaway. These templates are simple life application phrases that are used in spiritual growth. Adapt them to your particular devotional.

Is it cheating to use templates for takeaways? No. Like following the standard 3-part format for writing devotionals, it's smart. Templates offer patterns that have proven to work over time.

In fact, you can see how the takeaway from the example above is based on a template:

Template: What is [an attitude you can adopt] towards [a person or circumstance]?

Takeaway: How is God prompting you to [adopt an attitude of grace] towards [your in-laws]?

A Few Examples

Here are a few examples of takeaway templates. (Get the full list of Templates for Takeaways in Appendix D.)

What is [an attitude to adopt] [towards a person or circumstance]?

What is [a challenge to face] about [a person or circumstance]?

What [change] can you make to [do something or take a specific action]?

What [condition] is God calling you to meet about [a situation, person, or topic]?

[What or How] is God calling you [to face or to avoid] [a specific sin]?

Write Several Takeaways — and Choose One

You may want to write several takeaways for your devotional, each based on a different template. Then you can choose one.

Let's say you're writing a set of devotionals for children who are getting ready to or have just become older siblings. You write a short illustration about a girl who is going to be a big sister, describing the ways she helps her mom get ready for the new baby. The devotional is based on Matthew 3:3, in which John the Baptist, Jesus' cousin, helped people get ready for the coming Messiah. John the Baptist knew that Jesus was coming. The girl in your story knew the baby was coming. John helped people get ready. The girl helps her mother and father get ready. Some people got angry that John said a new king was coming. Would the girl get angry ... or would she be part of a good transition?

You could write several different kinds of takeaways for this devotional and then choose one that zeros in on the One Point:

- What can I do to help prepare for my new brother or sister? (A challenge to face)
- What is exciting and good about a new baby brother or sister? (A view to embrace)
- What uncertain feelings do I have about the new baby? Talk about them with a grown up friend. (A conflict to resolve, a mistake to prevent, or a sin to avoid)
- Think of a friend who is a big brother or big sister. What does he (or she) do that shows love to her younger sibling? (An example to follow)

- Ask God to show you how to be ready to be a big brother or big sister. (A prayer to pray.)

More Tips for Writing Takeaways

Take note of a few particulars that are specific to writing takeaways.

Use Strong Verbs

Takeaways are framed with verbs: "a conflict to **resolve**" ... "a promise to **claim**." There is a good reason for that: verbs are action words. Your takeaway challenges the reader to action. When writing your takeaway, use action words — verbs.

Consider Both Internal and External Applications

Takeaways can prompt external action (such as reaching out to a family member) or internal action (such as changing a thought pattern.) Action is action, whether it takes place on the outside or the inside.

Avoid "Yes" or "No" Takeaways

As you write your takeaway, do so by using open-ended questions or statements. The point is to get the reader to personalize the takeaway. If the takeaway can be answered with a simple "yes" or "no," then re-phrase it. Tip: use how, what, or why to ask takeaway questions.

Use the Most Appropriate Format

Will you format your takeaway as a prayer? A memory verse? A task? A question to ponder? Know how the publication for which you're writing prefers to challenge readers to take the next step. If you are publishing your own devotionals (whether in print or online), then choose how you will structure your takeaway to have the most impact for your target demographic group.

Use the Most Appropriate Point of View

If you are writing for a specific publication, be aware of how it structures viewpoint in the takeaway section. Some prefer first person ("Today, I will …") and some use second person ("Today, how will you …?")

Use the Most Appropriate Length

The takeaway is usually short — about 25-50 words at most. If you've done a good job in the illustration section, then you won't need more space than that to challenge the reader to action because you'll have already made your point. All that is left is to personalize it.

Try This

Always run your final takeaway through your standard S-A-M checklist:

- Is it simple? Remember — devotionals are just one small tool in the spiritual growth tool box. Keep your takeaway brief and to the point.

- Is it authentic? Give the reader a practical step to take that he can implement in real life.
- Is it memorable? You want the reader to store the takeaway on her mental hard drive and pull it up from time to time during the rest of the day, later in the week, or at some point down the road — so she will act upon it.

What a Takeaway Cannot Do

Lest you get overwhelmed by the impact of writing the takeaway, remember this: you cannot force the reader to change. Nor are you responsible for the reader putting the devotional truth into practice.

Only God can do that.

However, you are responsible for offering a challenge through your devotional in the best way you possibly can.

A strong takeaway can be the nudge your reader needs. One that sticks.

16

STICKY EXTRAS

In addition to the standard three parts in a devotional (scripture, illustration, takeaway), some devos employ extra elements.

Extras can add to a presentation or spotlight the point you want to make. You want to know a bit about these extras so you can include them when your publisher requires them or when you write for a particular genre (such as for children.) Or perhaps as you create your own devotionals, you choose to add additional elements as part of your distinctive style.

These are the most commonly-used extras ... and how to make sure they are sticky.

Most Common Extras Used in Devotionals

Title

Your devotional's title is an "extra essential." You need to write one. The best devotional titles grab the reader's attention and get her to keep reading, either by rousing her curiosity, summarizing the One Point, or promising a benefit or result. (See Appendix E for types of titles to use as you name your devotional.)

Main Point

Sometimes called a "Growth Point" or simply "The Point," this short, pithy statement summarizes the devotional's key principle. It encapsulates the One Point your devotional conveys.

If you've followed the One Point Rule, then this element is a simple matter of cut-and-paste. As we discussed in Chapter 12, it is a good practice to write out your main point and adhere to it as you create your devotional, regardless of whether or not you use it as an element in your devotional.

Theme

When you write a group of devotionals that follow a theme, indicate it in the header, such as "Forgiveness," "Purity," or "Thanksgiving."

This allows the reader to understand that they can explore the theme further through other devos. If you post the devotional online, be sure to list the theme as a keyword.

"Read More" Section

Your devo may spark interest and move your reader to want to investigate the topic further. You may choose to offer materials to help her do so. A "Read More" section can list related scripture, related devotionals, or related articles — all linked online or referenced by the publisher if in print.

Questions

Some devotionals offer a series of three or four questions in the takeaway, rather than just one. Questions are particularly helpful when devotionals are used in groups, presented in a series, or when they address a complex topic needing deeper understanding. A devotional with extra questions is a hybrid form that can become a bridge to a Bible study for individual readers or groups.

Activity

Puzzles, games, or simple crafts are typical extras offered in children's devotionals.

Do's and Don'ts for Extras

Do Treat Extras as Extra

If you include these elements, make sure they are true to their name. They are extra, not essential. The devotional should be able to stand alone and stick without the extras.

Don't Let Extras Detract

Don't let any extras undermine the 3-part devotional structure. If your questions or related scripture are more substantial than the devotional message, then you're writing a Bible study (not a devotional). If your focus for your 8-year-old reader is the craft, then you're writing a set of craft instructions (not a devotional.)

Don't Add Another Point

Remember the One Point Rule: to be sticky, a devotional makes just one spiritual point. If you add extra elements to your devotional, make sure they reinforce the single point you make. Don't give into the temptation to sneak in another spiritual insight.

Try This

As always, run your extras through the S-A-M checklist.

- Is it simple? Keep your extras brief and on point.
- Is it authentic? Make sure the extra enhances the devotional's realism.
- Is it memorable? You want the extras to build upon the devotional's One Point by appealing to the senses or invoking emotions.

EPILOGUE: MAKE IT STICK

———

17

MAKE IT STICK

THIS BOOK HAS TAKEN YOU THROUGH THE PROCESS OF writing devotionals — short, inspiring illustrations each with a biblical takeaway — so they stay with today's busy, distracted readers.

You'll recall that our approach was based on this biblical blueprint: "Write the vision; make it plain on tablets, so he may run who reads it" (Habakkuk 2:2).

We've drawn our step-by-step process from God's instructions to the prophet Habakkuk, showing how to:

- Become a stickable writer who can identify a truth about God from your daily life, capture it, and process it
- Understand your reader's stickability and write to it
- Use tools to choose one point per devotional and then write each of a devotional's three elements in a way that is simple, authentic, and memorable to make that point.

The goal of this book was not simply to equip you to write devotionals.

Rather, the goal was to equip you write devotionals that stick to your readers, so they can draw upon snippets of truth in the midst of their hectic, demanding lives — and grow.

What Next?

If you read the rest of Habakkuk, you'll discover something interesting. He writes:

"Yet I will rejoice in the Lord;

I will take joy in the God of my salvation.

God, the Lord, is my strength." (Habakkuk 3:18-19)

The entire final chapter of Habakkuk is a song of praise.

This from a man who had observed death and destruction ... saw decay of the culture around him ... challenged God ... wrestled with his fear and doubts ... and who faced the reality of upcoming destruction.

He kept talking to God. He listened to God's answers. In the end, Habakkuk worshipped.

What About You?

In many ways we are like Habakkuk. We experience conflict. We see struggles people face. We wonder where God is in the midst of those challenges.

You and I are much like those around us. We have active, full days. Our to-do lists are packed. All kinds of people and needs demand our attention.

In the midst of your writing journey, may I encourage you to take one more tip from the good prophet.

Do what he did: keep talking to God. Keep listening to how He answers. And in the end, keep praising Him.

The truth is that God is worthy of that praise.

That's the best way to make sure God's truth sticks to others: Make sure it sticks to you.

APPENDIX A: WHERE TO LOOK FOR IDEAS

Ideas for devotionals can come from any incident, person, situation, comment, example, anecdote, quote, statistic, fact, mannerism, activity, happening ... anything that grabs your attention. Here are some places to look to get started.

- "Ah ha" moments
- Births and deaths
- Buildings
- Chores and housekeeping
- Conversations
- Current events
- Daydreams
- Decisions
- Embarrassing moments
- Facts and statistics
- Food and meals
- Historical events
- Holidays
- Illnesses

- Interesting experiences
- Junk mail
- Memories
- Mind maps
- Mistakes
- Movies
- Music
- Nature and the outdoors
- Newspapers and magazines
- Paintings and cartoons
- People
- Quotes
- Sermons, lectures, classes
- Shopping
- Short stories, books, novels
- Social media
- Sports
- Television programs and commercials
- Trends
- Trivia

APPENDIX B: CREATE A READER PROFILE

Use this checklist to get started creating a reader profile of the typical person who will read your devotional.

- How old is your reader?
- What is your reader's gender?
- What is your reader's citizenship?
- What is your reader's marital status?
- Describe your reader's family.
- What is your reader's level of education?
- How is your reader employed?
- What is your reader's annual income?
- Does your reader own his own home?
- What are your reader's political views?
- What are your reader's hobbies?
- What are your reader's other interests?
- What does your reader care about?
- What causes does your reader support?

- Is your reader a Christ-follower, a seeker, a non-believer, or does he hold another religious view?
- Does your reader go to church?
- How much does your reader know about the Bible?
- How often does your reader read the Bible?
- What else does your reader read?
- List additional unique characteristics about your reader.

APPENDIX C: PUBLISHING RESOURCES

Print-On-Demand Providers
> CreateSpace
> Ingram Spark
> LightningSource
> Blurb

Independent Publishing Providers: Do It Yourself
> Kindle (KDP)
> Kobo
> NookPress
> iTunes Connect
> Smashwords
> BookBaby
> Draft 2Digital

Independent Publishing Providers: Full- or Partial-Service
> CreateSpace
> BookBaby

Smashwords
Ebook Architects
Bibliocrunch

APPENDIX D: TEMPLATES FOR TAKEAWAYS

- What is [an attitude to adopt] towards [a person or circumstance]?
- What is [a challenge to face] about [a person or circumstance]?
- What [change] can you make to [specific action]?
- What [condition] can you meet about [situation, person, or topic]?
- What [conflict] to resolve with [person or circumstance]?
- What [detail] can you consider about [situation, person, or topic]?
- What [example to follow] do you find in [situation, person, or topic]?
- How can you come to [forgive, reconcile] the [hurt] you experienced [time, place]?
- What [idea] can you pursue to [specific action]?
- Name the [lie] exposed here and the [truth] that is real.

- What [mistake] can you prevent about [situation, person, or topic]?
- What prayer can you pray about [situation, person, or topic]?
- Is there a [command] to obey about [situation, person, or topic]?
- What promise can you claim about [situation, person, or topic]?
- In [what area] can you build your relationship with [situation, person, or topic]?
- What scripture can you study further to learn more about [topic]?
- [What or How] is God calling you [to face or to avoid] [a specific sin]?
- What [thought, idea] can you ponder about [situation, person, or topic] in order to [action]?
- Name the [truth] you are called to face about [situation, person, or topic].
- What [verse] can you memorize to strengthen your [area of faith life]?
- What [view] are you to embrace about [situation, person, or topic] — and why?
- What [virtue] can you to cultivate and [what step] can you take first?

APPENDIX E: TYPES OF TITLES

Your devotional's title has an important job: it needs to attract a reader's attention and get him to keep reading. Try these types of titles to attract your reader's attention with the title.

- Summarize the point
- Identify the audience
- Announce news
- Offer a benefit
- Ask a provocative question
- Give a command
- Provide useful information
- Explain how to
- Explain secrets
- Explain reasons why
- Present a problem and its solution
- Do (something) fast
- Do (something) easier
- Show a cause — effect (If ... Then)
- Summarize the content

INDEX OF SCRIPTURE REFERENCES

ACKNOWLEDGMENTS

Special thanks to my husband Brett, daughter Britta, and son Kurt for their unwavering support and encouragement; to my beta readers Kim Frost, Nancy Pennington, and Rachel Wilmot for their editorial input; and for the dozens of early readers who provided feedback and reviews.

To my readers: thank you for your enthusiasm! And yes, I would love to speak at your event or gathering. Please find me on my website and blog, Word Wise at Nonprofit Copywriter (www.nonprofitcopywriter.com).

If you enjoyed this book, please consider writing a review on Amazon, BN.com, or GoodReads. This way more writers and writers-to-be can learn to write devotionals that stick! (A great way to build the Kingdom, by the way.)

ABOUT THE AUTHOR

Kathy Widenhouse is a content writer who specializes in writing for faith-based organizations and the nonprofit market.

She was always been a reader, but began writing in earnest in 1996 when planning for a second career after serving in the military. (Kathy spent 20 years as a flutist with "The President's Own" U.S. Marine Band in Washington, D.C., before turning to writing full-time.) A letter in her mailbox invited her to take an online article-writing course. Soon she was earning periodical bylines and book contracts. When Kathy turned to content and copywriting, her years of volunteer work and time on four nonprofit boards drew her to the nonprofit niche.

As she began partnering with small to mid-sized organizations as a development writer and a freelance Christian writer, Kathy discovered that many of them struggle in the communications arena — most often because staff members wear too many hats. She learned that by providing good information and reliable service for these committed professionals, they are able to develop effective communications, build their donor base, and grow.

Along the way, 100+ articles with Kathy's byline have appeared in more than 40 periodicals, both print and online, and her 5 books now number more than 100,000 in print. Today, she invests time as an online information publisher and in helping nonprofits, entrepreneurs, and ministries have great writing for their organizations.

She and her husband Brett have two terrific grown children. They live in Lake Wylie, SC. And she is still a reader.

For more information:

www.nonprofitcopywriter.com
kathy@nonprofitcopywriter.com

MORE FROM KATHY WIDENHOUSE

God and Me! 3 *(Ages 6-9)*

One of the newest additions to the publisher's best-selling series for girls, *God and Me!* 3 is filled with devotionals based on The Lord's Prayer. The book is packed with fun, Bible-based stories and activities that equip girls to grow closer to God and discover His promises for their lives.

God and Me! 3 *(Ages 10-12)*
One of the newest additions to the publisher's best-selling series for pre-teen girls, *God and Me!* 3 is filled with devotionals based on The Ten Commandments. The book is packed with fun, Bible-based stories and activities that equip girls to grow closer to God and discover His promises for their lives.

The Christian Girl's Guide to Friendship
This book's fun, magazine-style format makes it easy for pre-teen girls to get a good start having fantastic friends and being one, too.

The Un-Santa Book
This book is packed with fun ideas for celebrating the gift of God's Son and meaningful Christmas activities in an outreach event at your church, with your homeschool group, with friends and neighbors, and in your home!

The Un-Bunny Book
This book is packed with fun ideas for celebrating the Resurrection and meaningful Easter activities in an outreach event at your church, with your homeschool group, with friends and neighbors, and in your home!

———

31525683R00096

Printed in Great Britain
by Amazon